The Little MLer

The Little MLer

Matthias Felleisen

Rice University
Houston, Texas

Daniel P. Friedman

Indiana University
Bloomington, Indiana

Drawings by Duane Bibby

Foreword by Robin Milner

The MIT Press
Cambridge, Massachusetts
London, England

This book was set by the authors and was printed and bound in the United States of America.

Library of Congress Cataloging-in-Publication Data

Felleisen, Matthias
The little MLer / Matthias Felleisen and Daniel P. Friedman; drawings by Duane Bibby; foreword by Robin Milner
p. cm.
Includes index and bibliographical references.
ISBN 0-262-56114-X (pbk : alk. paper)
1. ML (Computer program language) I. Friedman, Daniel P. II. Title.
QA76.73.M6F45 1998
005.13′3—dc21 97-40550
CIP

To Helga, Christopher, and Sebastian.
To Mary, Rob, Rachel, Sara,
and to the memory of Brian.

Contents

Foreword

This is a book about writing programs, and understanding them as you write them. Most large computer programs are never completely understood; if they were, they wouldn't go wrong so often and we would be able to describe what they do in a scientific way. A good language should help to improve this state of affairs.

There are many ways of trying to understand programs. People often rely too much on one way, which is called "debugging" and consists of running a partly-understood program to see if it does what you expected. Another way, which ML advocates, is to install some means of understanding in the very programs themselves.

Standard ML was designed with this in mind. There are two particular ways-of-understanding built in to Standard ML; one is *types* for understanding data, the other is the *module system* for understanding the structure of the large-scale programs. People who program in a language with a strong type system, like this one, often say that their programs have fewer mistakes, and they understand them better.

The authors focus upon these features of Standard ML. They are well equipped to help you to understand programming; they are experienced teachers as well as researchers of the elegant and simple ideas which inspire good programming languages and good programming style.

Above all they have written a book which is a pleasure to read; it is free of heavy detail, but doesn't avoid tricky points. I hope you will enjoy the book and be able to use the ideas, whatever programming language you use in the future.

Robin Milner
Cambridge University

Preface

Programs consume data and produce data; designing a program requires a thorough understanding of data. In ML, programmers can express their understanding of the data using the sublanguage of types. Once the types are formulated, the design of the program follows naturally. Its shape will reflect the shape of the types and type definitions. Most collections of data, and hence most type specifications, are inductive, that is, they are defined in terms of themselves. Hence, most programs are recursive; again, they are defined in terms of themselves.

The first and primary goal of this book is to teach you to think recursively about types and programs. Perhaps the best programming language for understanding types and recursive thinking is ML. It has a rich, practical type language, and recursion is its natural computational mechanism. Since our primary concern is the idea of recursion, our treatment of ML in the first eight chapters is limited to the whys and wherefores of just a few features: types, datatypes, and functions.

The second goal of this book is to expose you to two important topics concerning large programs: dealing with exceptional situations and composing program components. Managing exceptional situtations is possible, but awkward, with recursive functions. Consequently, ML provides a small and pragmatic sublanguage, *i.e.*, **exception**, **raise**, and **handle**, for dealing with such situations. The exception mechanism can also be used as a control tool to simplify recursive definitions when appropriate.

Typically, programs consist of many collections of many types and functions. Each collection is a progam component or module. Constructing large programs means combining modules but also requires understanding the dependencies among the components. ML supports a powerful sublanguage for that purpose. In the last chapter, we introduce you to this language and the art of combining program components. The module sublanguage is again a functional programming language, just like the one we present in the first eight chapters, but its basic values are modules (called structures) not integers or booleans.

While *The Little MLer* provides an introduction to the principles of types, computation, and program construction, you should also know that ML itself is more general and incorporates more than we could intelligibly cover in an introductory text. After you have mastered this book, you can read and understand more advanced and comprehensive books on ML.

Acknowledgments

We are indebted to Benjamin Pierce for numerous readings and insightful suggestions on improving the presentation and to Robert Harper for criticisms of the book and guidance concerning the new module system of ML. Michael Ashley, Cynthia Brown, Robby Findler, Matthew Flatt, Jeremy Frens, Steve Ganz, Daniel Grossman, Erik Hilsdale, Julia Lawall, Shinn-Der Lee, Michael Levin, David MacQueen, Kevin Millikin, Jon Riecke, George Springer, and Mitchell Wand read the book at various stages of development and their comments helped produce the final result. We also wish to thank Robert Prior at MIT Press who loyally supported us for many years. The book greatly benefited from Dorai Sitaram's incredibly clever Scheme typesetting program SLaTeX. Finally, we would like to thank the National Science Foundation for its continued support and especially for the Educational Innovation Grant that provided us with the opportunity to collaborate for the past year.

What You Need to Know to Read This Book

You must be comfortable reading English and performing rudimentary arithmetic. A willingness to use paper and pencil to ensure understanding is absolutely necessary.

Reading Guidelines

Do not rush through this book. Read carefully; valuable hints are scattered throughout the text. Do not read the first eight chapters in fewer than three sittings. Allow one sitting at least for each of the last two chapters. Read systematically. If you do not *fully* understand one chapter, you will understand the next one even less.

The book is a dialogue about interesting examples of ML programs. If you can, try the examples while you read. Since ML implementations are predominantly interactive, the programmer can immediately participate in and observe the behavior of expressions. We encourage you to use this interactive read-evaluate-and-print loop to experiment with our definitions and examples. Some hints concerning experimentation are provided below.

We do not give any formal definitions in this book. We believe that you can form your own definitions and thus remember and understand them better than if we had written them out for you. But be sure you know and understand the morals that appear at the end of each chapter.

We use a few notational conventions throughout the text, primarily changes in typeface for different classes of symbols. Variables are in *italic*. Basic data, including numbers, booleans, constructors introduced via datatypes, are set in sans serif. Keywords, e.g., **datatype**, **of**, **and**, **fun**, are in **boldface**. When you experiment with the programs, you may ignore the typefaces but not the related framenotes. To highlight this role of typefaces, the ML fragments in framenotes are set in a `typewriter` face.

Food appears in many of our examples for two reasons. First, food is easier to visualize than abstract ideas. (This is not a good book to read while dieting.) We hope the choice of food will help you understand the examples and concepts we use. Second, we want to provide you with a little distraction. We know how frustrating the subject matter can be, and a little distraction will help you keep your sanity.

You are now ready to start. Good luck! We hope you will enjoy the experiences waiting for you on the following pages.

Bon appétit!

Matthias Felleisen
Daniel P. Friedman

Experimenting with SML

The book's programming language is a small subset of SML. With minor modifications, the examples of the first nine chapters of the book will run on most implementations of SML. For the tenth chapter, an implementation based on the 1996/97 revision of SML must be used.

The best mode to conduct experiments is

1. to place `Compiler.Control.Print.printDepth := 20;` into a newly created file,
2. to append the desired definitions (boxes) to the file,
3. to add a semicolon after each box, and
4. to employ `use "<filename>";` to load the definitions into the read-eval-print loop.

SML is then ready to accept and evaluate expressions that refer to the new definitions.

Experimenting with Objective Caml

Objective Caml is a major dialect of the family of ML languages. The best mode to conduct experiments with Objective Caml is

1. to place `#print_depth 20;;` into a newly created file,
2. to append the desired definitions (boxes) to the file,
3. to add *two* semicolons after each box, and
4. to employ `#use "<filename>";;` to load the definitions into the read-eval-print loop.

Objective Caml is then ready to accept and evaluate expressions that refer to the new definitions.

Objective Caml's syntax differs slightly from SML's. By using the following hints systematically, you can easily translate the boxes from the first nine chapters of the book into Objective Caml. Each hint is marked by a chapter number and a frame number. If you are using Objective Caml, annotate the corresponding frames before you start reading to remind you where the differences between SML's and Objective Caml's syntaxes first appear.

1:16 Replace `datatype` by `type`:

```
type seasoning =
   Salt
 | Pepper
```

2:15 Replace `fun` by `let rec` and use `function`. The patterns omit the function name:

```
let rec only_onions =
  function
    (Skewer)
    -> true
  | (Onion(x))
    -> only_onions(x)
  | (Lamb(x))
    -> false
  | (Tomato(x))
    -> false
```

4:66 To specify the precise types that a function should consume and produce, wrap the function name with the type assertion:

```
let rec (has_steak : meza * main * dessert -> bool) =
  function
    (x,Steak,d)
    -> true
  | (x,ns,d)
    -> false
```

7:11 Since constructors are not functions in Objective Caml, define **hot_maker** as follows:

```
let rec hot_maker(x) =
  function
    (x)
    -> Hot(x)
```

8:93 Curried definitions with matching on the first consumed value need parentheses around the function being returned when the second consumed value is placed in parentheses as we do here:

```
let rec combine_c =
  function
    (Empty)
    -> (function
          (l2)
          -> l2)
  | (Cons(a,l1))
    -> (function
          (l2)
          -> Cons(a,combine_c(l1)(l2)))
```

9:14 Replace `No_bacon 0` by `(No_bacon 0)`.

9:84 Replace (exp_1 **handle** *pattern* => exp_2) by (**try** exp_1 **with** *pattern* -> exp_2).

Also, replace `div` by `/`:

```
let rec find(n,boxes) =
  (try check(n,boxes,list_item(n,boxes))
    with
     Out_of_range
     -> find(n / 2,boxes))
and check =
  function
    (n,boxes,Bacon)
    -> n
  | (n,boxes,Ix(i))
    -> find(i,boxes)
```

10 The examples of this chapter can be expressd in Objective Caml, but see the manual for the syntax of modules and simple examples that use them before you do.

The Little MLer

1. Building Blocks

Is this a number: 5?	1	Yes.
Is 5 also an integer?	2	Yes, it is.
Is this a number: 17?	3	Yes, it is also an integer.
Is this a number: ~23?	4	Yes, but we don't use negative integers.
Is this an integer: 5.32?	5	No, and we don't use reals.
What type of number is 5?	6	*int*.[1] [1] The symbol *int* stands for "integer."
Quick, think of another integer!	7	How about 13?
What type of value is true?	8	*bool*.[1] [1] The symbol *bool* stands for "boolean."
What type of value is false?	9	*bool*.
Can you think of another *bool*?	10	No, that's all there is to *bool*.
Are there more *int*s than *bool*s?	11	Lots.
What is *int*?	12	A type.
What is *bool*?	13	Another type.

What is a type?

14 A type is a name for a collection of values.

What is a type?

15 Sometimes we use it as if it were the collection.

Does this define a new type?

```
datatype seasoning =
   Salt
 | Pepper
```

16 Yes, it does.

Is this a *seasoning*: Salt?

17 Yes, it is.

And Pepper?

18 It's also a *seasoning*.

Can you think of another *seasoning*?

19 No, there are two. And that's all.

Have we seen a type like *seasoning* before?

20 Yes, *bool* also has just two values.

Does this define a new type, too?

```
datatype num =
   Zero
 | One_more_than of num
```

21 Yes, it does.

Is this a *num*: Zero?

22 Obviously, just like Salt is a *seasoning*.

Is One_more_than(Zero) a *num*?

23 Yes, because One_more_than constructs a *num* from a *num*.

How does One_more_than do that?

24 We gave it Zero, which is a *num*, and it constructs a new *num*.

What is the type of

```
One_more_than(
  One_more_than(
    Zero))?
```

25 *num*, because One_more_than constructs a *num* from a *num* and we agreed that

```
One_more_than(
  Zero)
```

is a *num*.

What is

```
One_more_than(
  0)?
```

26 This is *nonsense*,[1] because 0 is not a *num*.

[1] We use the word "nonsense" for an expression that has no type.

What is the type of

```
One_more_than(
  One_more_than(
    One_more_than(
      One_more_than(
        Zero))))?
```

27 *num*.

What is the difference between Zero and 0?

28 The value Zero belongs to the type *num*, whereas 0 belongs to *int*.

Correct. In general, if two things belong to two different types, they cannot be the same.

29 A type is a name for a collection of values, and there is no overlap for any two distinct types.

Are there more *nums* than *bools*?

30 Lots.

Are there more *nums* than *ints*?

31 No.[1]

[1] And we will see in a later chapter why there are as many *ints* as *nums*.

What does this define?

```
datatype α¹ open_faced_sandwich =
    Bread of α
  | Slice of α open_faced_sandwich
```

[1] We use 'a for α, but it is pronounced alpha.

32 It looks like the definition of a new type, but it also contains this funny looking α.

What is Bread(0)?

33 It looks like an element of

α open_faced_sandwich.

And what is Bread(true)?

34 It also looks like an element of

α open_faced_sandwich.

But how can both Bread(0) and Bread(true) be elements of the same type?

They can't! They belong to two different types:

int open_faced_sandwich

and

bool open_faced_sandwich.

35 What does that mean?

It means that

```
datatype α open_faced_sandwich =
    Bread of α
  | Slice of α open_faced_sandwich
```

is not a type definition but a shape that represents many different datatypes.

36 Okay, that makes sense.

So, if we write *int open_faced_sandwich*, we mean a type like this.[1]

```
datatype int open_faced_sandwich =
   Bread of int
 | Slice of int open_faced_sandwich        ⊗
```

What does *bool open_faced_sandwich* mean?

[1] The marker ⊗ indicates that this definition is ungrammatical. We use this ungrammatical definition to explain α *open_faced_sandwich*.

37 Writing *bool open_faced_sandwich* is as if we had defined a new **datatype**.

```
datatype bool open_faced_sandwich =
   Bread of bool
 | Slice of bool open_faced_sandwich        ⊗
```

So what is *int open_faced_sandwich*?

38 The simplest way of saying "This is an instance of the definition of

α *open_faced_sandwich*

where α stands for *int*."

And what is *bool open_faced_sandwich*?

39 The simplest way of saying "This is an instance of the definition of

α *open_faced_sandwich*

where α stands for *bool*."

What is *num open_faced_sandwich*?

40 The simplest way of saying "This is an instance of the definition of

α *open_faced_sandwich*

where α stands for *num*."

Does that also mean that we can derive as many types as we want from the shape

α *open_faced_sandwich*?

41 Yes.

Is

```
Bread(0)
```

an

int open_faced_sandwich?

42 Yes.

Why does it belong to
int open_faced_sandwich
and not
bool open_faced_sandwich?

43 Because 0 is an *int*, and Bread constructs elements of type *int open_faced_sandwich* when it is given an *int*.

And what is the type of Bread(true)?

44 *bool open_faced_sandwich*.

To what type does

```
Bread(
  One_more_than(
    Zero))
```

belong?

45 It belongs to *num open_faced_sandwich*.

Is

```
Bread(Bread(0))
```

an
(*int open_faced_sandwich*)
open_faced_sandwich?

46 Yes, because *int open_faced_sandwich* is a type, and we said that we can derive a new type from α *open_faced_sandwich* by replacing α with any type.

And finally, since (*num open_faced_sandwich*) is also a type, to what type does

```
Bread(
  Bread(
    One_more_than(
      Zero)))
```

belong?

47 It belongs to
(*num open_faced_sandwich*)
open_faced_sandwich.

Wow, types are types.

The First Moral

Use datatype to describe types. When a type contains lots of values, the datatype definition refers to itself. Use α with datatype to define shapes.

2.
Matchmaker, Matchmaker

Here is another type definition.

```
datatype shish_kebab =
  Skewer
| Onion of shish_kebab
| Lamb of shish_kebab
| Tomato of shish_kebab
```

What is different about it?

1 It contains four alternatives, not just two.

What is an element of this new type?

2 How about
Skewer?

And another one?

3 Here's one:

```
Onion(
  Skewer).
```

And a third?

4 Here's one more:

```
Onion(
  Lamb(
    Onion(
      Skewer))).
```

Are there only Onions on this *shish_kebab:*
Skewer?

5 true, because there is neither Lamb nor Tomato on the Skewer.

Are there only Onions on this *shish_kebab:*

```
Onion(
  Skewer)?
```

6 true.

And how about:

```
Lamb(
  Skewer)?
```

7 false, it contains Lamb.

Is it true that

```
Onion(
  Onion(
    Onion(
      Skewer)))
```

contains only Onions?

8 true.

And finally:

```
Onion(
  Lamb(
    Onion(
      Skewer)))?
```

9 false.

Is it true that

```
5
```

contains only Onions?

10 What kind of question is that? That looks like nonsense, because 5 is an *int*, not a *shish_kebab*.

Write the function *only_onions* using **fun**, =, |, (,), true, false, Skewer, Onion, Lamb, and Tomato.

11 Of course, you can't write this function, yet. Okay, you deserve something sweet for enduring this last question.

What kind of things does *only_onions* consume?

12 *shish_kebab*s.

And what does it produce?

13 *bool*s.

Are you anxious to see the first function definition?

14 Yes, we can't wait for the next page.

Here it is.

```
fun only_onions(Skewer)
    = true
  | only_onions(Onion(x))
    = only_onions(x)
  | only_onions(Lamb(x))
    = false
  | only_onions(Tomato(x))
    = false
```

```
only_onions[1] :
  shish_kebab → bool
                              •
```

Did you notice the second box?

[1] This box (type assertion) is a part of the program. It is transcribed as

```
(only_onions : shish_kebab -> bool)
```

so that implementations can verify your thoughts about the type of a function. The transcription must always follow the function definition, never precede it. In general, if a box contains a bullet •, then you must transcribe it by putting a left parenthesis in front of the contents and a right parenthesis behind it. The arrow is transcribed with two characters: - followed by >.

15 Yes, the second box is not a function definition. Why is the second box there?

The second box states what *only_onions* consumes and produces.

16 What is in front of (*i.e.*, to the left of) the symbol → is the type of things that the function consumes, and what is behind → is the type of things it produces.

Is

shish_kebab → *bool*

the type of *only_onions*?

17 Yes, *shish_kebab* → *bool* is the type of *only_onions* just as *int* is the type of 5.

Which item is mentioned first in the definition of *shish_kebab*?

18 Skewer.

Which item is mentioned first in the definition of *only_onions*?

19 Skewer.

---

20 Which item is mentioned second in the definition of *shish_kebab*?

Onion.

21 Which item is mentioned second in the definition of *only_onions*?

Onion.

22 Does the sequence of items in the **datatype** definition correspond to the sequence in which they appear in the **fun**ction definition?

Yes, it does. Is this always the case?

23 Almost always.

Okay.

24 What is the value of

```
only_onions(
  Onion(
    Onion(
      Skewer)))?
```

true.

25 And how do we determine the answer of

```
only_onions(
  Onion(
    Onion(
      Skewer)))?
```

We will need to pay attention to the function definition.

```
fun only_onions(Skewer)
      = true
  | only_onions(Onion(x))
      = only_onions(x)
  | only_onions(Lamb(x))
      = false
  | only_onions(Tomato(x))
      = false
```

26 Does

```
only_onions(
  Onion(
    Onion(
      Skewer)))
```

match

```
only_onions(Skewer)?
```

No.

Why not?

27 Because
Onion(
  Onion(
    Skewer))
does not match Skewer.

Does
only_onions(
  Onion(
    Onion(
      Skewer)))
match
only_onions(Onion(x))?

28 Yes, if x stands for
Onion(
  Skewer).

Let x stand for
Onion(
  Skewer).

29 In that case, we have found a match.

Then what is
only_onions(
  Onion(
    Skewer))?

30 It is
only_onions(x),
which is what follows the '=' below *only_onions*(Onion(x)) in the definition of *only_onions*, with x replaced by what it stands for:
Onion(
  Skewer).

Why do we need to know the meaning of
only_onions(
  Onion(
    Skewer))?

31 Because the answer for
only_onions(
  Onion(
    Skewer))
is also the answer for
only_onions(
  Onion(
    Onion(
      Skewer))).

How do we determine the answer of
only_onions(
Onion(
Skewer))?

32 Let's see.

Does
only_onions(
Onion(
Skewer))
match
only_onions(Skewer)?

33 No.

Why not?

34 Because
Onion(
Skewer)
does not match Skewer.

Does
only_onions(
Onion(
Skewer))
match
only_onions(Onion(x))?

35 Yes, if x stands for Skewer, now.

So let x stand for Skewer, now.

36 In that case, we have found our match again.

Then what is *only_onions*(Skewer)?

37 It is
only_onions(x),
which is what follows the '=' below *only_onions*(Onion(x)) in the definition of *only_onions*, with x replaced by what it stands for:
Skewer.

Why do we need to know what the meaning of

only_onions(Skewer)

is?

38 Because the answer for

only_onions(Skewer)

is the answer for

```
only_onions(
  Onion(
    Skewer)),
```

which is the answer for

```
only_onions(
  Onion(
    Onion(
      Skewer))).
```

How do we determine the answer of

only_onions(Skewer)?

39 We need to match one more time.

Does

only_onions(Skewer)

match

only_onions(Skewer)?

40 Completely.

Then what is the answer?

41 true.

Are we done?

42 Yes! The answer for

```
only_onions(
  Onion(
    Onion(
      Skewer)))
```

is the same as the answer for

```
only_onions(
  Onion(
    Skewer)),
```

which is the same as the answer for

only_onions(Skewer),

which is

true.

43 What is the answer of

```
only_onions(
  Onion(
    Lamb(
      Skewer)))?
```

false, isn't it?

---

44 Does

```
only_onions(
  Onion(
    Lamb(
      Skewer)))
```

match

```
only_onions(Skewer)?
```

No, it does not match.

---

45 Why not?

Because

```
Onion(
  Lamb(
    Skewer))
```

does not match Skewer.

---

46 Does

```
only_onions(
  Onion(
    Lamb(
      Skewer)))
```

match

```
only_onions(Onion(x))?
```

Yes, if x now stands for

```
Lamb(
  Skewer).
```

---

47 Next let x stand for

```
Lamb(
  Skewer).
```

In that case, they match.

Then what is *only_onions*(Lamb(Skewer))?	48 It is *only_onions*(x), which is what follows the '=' below *only_onions*(Onion(x)), with x replaced by what it stands for: Lamb(Skewer).
Why do we need to know what *only_onions*(Lamb(Skewer)) is?	49 Because the answer for *only_onions*(Lamb(Skewer)) is the answer for *only_onions*(Onion(Lamb(Skewer))).
Does *only_onions*(Lamb(Skewer)) match *only_onions*(Skewer)?	50 No.
Does *only_onions*(Lamb(Skewer)) match *only_onions*(Onion(x))?	51 No.
Does *only_onions*(Lamb(Skewer)) match *only_onions*(Lamb(x))?	52 Yes, if x stands for Skewer, now

And now what is the answer?

53 false, because false follows the '=' below *only_onions*(Lamb(x)) in the definition of *only_onions*.

Are we done?

54 Yes! The answer for

```
only_onions(
  Onion(
    Lamb(
      Skewer)))
```

is the same as the answer for

```
only_onions(
  Lamb(
    Skewer)),
```

which is

false.

Describe the function *only_onions* in your own words.

55 Here are our words:
"*only_onions* consumes a *shish_kebab* and checks to see whether it is only edible by an onion lover."

Describe how the function *only_onions* accomplishes this.

56 Here are our words again:
"*only_onions* looks at each piece of the *shish_kebab* and, if it doesn't encounter Lamb or Tomato, it produces true."

So what is the value of
only_onions(5)?

57 Nonsense. We already said that 5 is an *int*, not a *shish_kebab*.

Is

```
Tomato(
  Skewer)?
```

an element of *shish_kebab*?

58 Yes.

Is
  Onion(
    Tomato(
      Skewer))
an element of *shish_kebab*?

59 Since
  Tomato(
    Skewer)
is an element of *shish_kebab*, we can also wrap an Onion around it.

And how about another Tomato?

60 Sure.

Is
  Tomato(
    Onion(
      Tomato(
        Skewer)))
a vegetarian shish kebab?

61 Of course, there is no Lamb in it.

Is
  Onion(
    Onion(
      Onion(
        Skewer)))
a vegetarian shish kebab?

62 Yes, it only contains Onions.

Define the function
  is_vegetarian :
    shish_kebab → *bool*,
which returns true if what it consumes does not contain Lamb.

63 Shouldn't the line for Tomatoes in this function be the same as the line for Onions?

```
fun is_vegetarian(Skewer)
    = true
  | is_vegetarian(Onion(x))
    = is_vegetarian(x)
  | is_vegetarian(Lamb(x))
    = false
  | is_vegetarian(Tomato(x))
    = is_vegetarian(x)
```

```
is_vegetarian :
  shish_kebab → bool
```

64 Yes, that's right. Let's move on. What does

```
datatype α shish =
    Bottom of α
  | Onion of α shish
  | Lamb of α shish
  | Tomato of α shish
```

define?

It defines a datatype that is similar in shape to *shish_kebab*.

---

65 Do the definitions of α *shish* and *shish_kebab* use the same names?

Yes, the names of the constructors are the same, but clearly from now on Onion constructs an α *shish* and no longer a *shish_kebab*.

---

66 What is different about the new datatype?

A *shish_kebab* is always on a Skewer, an α *shish* is placed on different kinds of Bottoms.

---

67 Here are some bottom objects.

```
datatype rod =
    Dagger
  | Fork
  | Sword
```

Are they good ones?

Sure, *rod shish* makes some form of shish kebab.

---

68 Think of another class of bottom objects.

We could move all of the food to various forms of plates.

```
datatype plate =
    Gold_plate
  | Silver_plate
  | Brass_plate
```

---

69 What is the type of

```
Onion(
  Tomato(
    Bottom(Dagger)))?
```

It belongs to *rod shish*.

Is
  Onion(
    Tomato(
      Bottom(Dagger)))
a vegetarian *rod shish*?

70 Sure it is. It only contains Tomatoes and Onions.

Does
  Onion(
    Tomato(
      Bottom(Gold_plate)))
belong to *plate shish*?

71 Sure, because Gold_plate is a *plate* and *plate* is used as a Bottom, and Tomatoes and Onions can be wrapped around Bottoms.

Is
  Onion(
    Tomato(
      Bottom(Gold_plate)))
a vegetarian shish kebab?

72 Sure it is. It is basically like
  Onion(
    Tomato(
      Bottom(Dagger)))
except that we have moved all the food from a Dagger to a Gold_plate.

Let's define the function

is_veggie **:** α *shish* $\rightarrow$ *bool*,

which checks whether a shish kebab contains only vegetarian foods, regardless of what Bottom it is in.

73 It only differs from *is_vegetarian* in one part.

```
fun is_veggie(Bottom(x))
    = true
  | is_veggie(Onion(x))
    = is_veggie(x)
  | is_veggie(Lamb(x))
    = false
  | is_veggie(Tomato(x))
    = is_veggie(x)
```

```
is_veggie :
  α shish → bool
```

This new function matches against arbitrary Bottoms, whereas *is_vegetarian* only matches against Skewers.

Let's determine the value of

```
is_veggie(
  Onion(
    Fork)).
```

74 This is nonsense.

Why?

75 Because Onion constructs *α shish* from *α shish*, which does not include Fork.

What is the value of

```
is_veggie(
  Onion(
    Tomato(
      Bottom(Dagger))))?
```

76 true.

What type of thing is

```
Onion(
  Tomato(
    Bottom(Dagger)))?
```

77 We said it belonged to the type *rod shish*.

What is the value of

```
is_veggie(
  Onion(
    Tomato(
      Bottom(Gold_plate))))?
```

78 It is true, too.

And what type of thing is

```
Onion(
  Tomato(
    Bottom(Gold_plate)))?
```

79 It belongs to the type *plate shish*, which has the same shape as *rod shish*, but is a distinct type.

But aren't both examples of *α shish*?

80 Yes, they are. The two types only differ in how *α* is replaced by a type.

How can *is_veggie* consume things that belong to different types?

81 Perhaps we should think of *is_veggie* as two functions.

What functions should we think about?

82 One function has the type

rod shish → *bool*

and the other one has the type

plate shish → *bool*.

Where else do the functions differ?

83 Nowhere—they are identical otherwise.

So this is how we could have written the function *is_veggie* for *shish*es on rods.

```
datatype rod =
   Dagger
 | Fork
 | Sword
```

```
fun is_veggie(Bottom(x))
     = true
  | is_veggie(Onion(x))
     = is_veggie(x)
  | is_veggie(Lamb(x))
     = false
  | is_veggie(Tomato(x))
     = is_veggie(x)
```

```
is_veggie :
  rod shish → bool
```

And how would we write the function *is_veggie* for *shish*es on plates?

84 All we have to change is the type of Bottom and the type of the function.

```
datatype plate =
   Gold_plate
 | Silver_plate
 | Brass_plate
```

```
fun is_veggie(Bottom(x))
     = true
  | is_veggie(Onion(x))
     = is_veggie(x)
  | is_veggie(Lamb(x))
     = false
  | is_veggie(Tomato(x))
     = is_veggie(x)
```

```
is_veggie :
  plate shish → bool
```

Whew, that's a lot of writing!

What type of value is

```
is_veggie(
  Onion(
    Tomato(
      Bottom(52))))?
```

85 *bool*.

86 What type of value is

```
is_veggie(
  Onion(
    Tomato(
      Bottom(
        One_more_than(Zero)))))?
```

bool.

87 What type of value is

```
is_veggie(
  Onion(
    Tomato(
      Bottom(false))))?
```

bool.

88 Does that mean *is_veggie* works for all five types: *rod shish*, *plate shish*, *int shish*, *num shish*, and *bool shish*?

Yes, and all other *shish* types that we could possibly think of.

89 What is the bottom object of

```
Onion(
  Tomato(
    Bottom(Dagger)))?
```

All the food is on a dagger.

90 What is the bottom object of

```
Onion(
  Tomato(
    Bottom(Gold_plate)))?
```

All the food is now on a gold plate.

91 What is the bottom object of

```
Onion(
  Tomato(
    Bottom(52)))?
```

All the food is on a 52.

92 What is the value of

```
what_bottom(
  Onion(
    Tomato(
      Bottom(Dagger))))?
```

Dagger.

93 What is the value of
what_bottom(
Onion(
Tomato(
Bottom(Gold_plate))))?

Gold_plate.

---

94 What is the value of
what_bottom(
Onion(
Tomato(
Bottom(52))))?

52.

---

95 So what type of value does *what_bottom* consume?

α *shish*, which means all types of *shish*es.

---

96 And what type of value does *what_bottom* produce?

It produces *rods*, *plates*, and *ints*. And it looks like it can produce a whole lot more.

---

97 Is there a simple way of saying what type of value it produces?

Here is our way:
"If α is a type and we use *what_bottom* on a value of type α *shish*, then the result is of type α."

---

98 How many variants of *shish*es must *what_bottom* match?

There are four.

```
fun what_bottom(Bottom(x))
  = ________
  | what_bottom(Onion(x))
  = ________
  | what_bottom(Lamb(x))
  = ________
  | what_bottom(Tomato(x))
  = ________
```

---

99 What is the value of
what_bottom(
Bottom(52))?

52.

---

100 What is the value of
what_bottom(
Bottom(Sword))?

Sword.

---

101 What is the value of
what_bottom(
Bottom(x)),
no matter what x is?

x.

---

102 So what goes into the first blank line of *what_bottom*?

x.

---

103 What is the value of
what_bottom(
Tomato(
Onion(
Lamb(
Bottom(52)))))?

52.

---

104 What is the value of
what_bottom(
Onion(
Lamb(
Bottom(52))))?

52.

---

105 What is the value of
what_bottom(
Lamb(
Bottom(52)))?

52.

---

106 What is the value of
what_bottom(
Bottom(52))?

52.

107 Does that mean that the value of

```
what_bottom(
  Tomato(
   Onion(
    Lamb(
     Bottom(52)))))
```

is the same as

```
what_bottom(
  Onion(
   Lamb(
    Bottom(52)))),
```

which is the same as

```
what_bottom(
  Lamb(
   Bottom(52))),
```

which is the same as

```
what_bottom(
  Bottom(52))?
```

Yes, all four have the same answer: 52.

---

108 Fill in the blanks in this skeleton.

```
fun what_bottom(Bottom(x))
    = x
  | what_bottom(Onion(x))
    = what_bottom(x)
  | what_bottom(Lamb(x))
    = ________
  | what_bottom(Tomato(x))
    = ________
```

Now this is easy.

```
fun what_bottom(Bottom(x))
    = x
  | what_bottom(Onion(x))
    = what_bottom(x)
  | what_bottom(Lamb(x))
    = what_bottom(x)
  | what_bottom(Tomato(x))
    = what_bottom(x)
```

```
what_bottom :
  α shish → α
```

The Second Moral

The number and order of the patterns in the definition of a function should match that of the definition of the consumed datatype.

3. Cons Is Still Magnificent

Do you like to eat pizza?

```
datatype pizza =
    Crust
  | Cheese of pizza
  | Onion of pizza
  | Anchovy of pizza
  | Sausage of pizza
```

1 Looks like good toppings.

Here is our favorite pizza:

```
Anchovy(
  Onion(
    Anchovy(
      Anchovy(
        Cheese(
          Crust))))).
```

2 This looks too salty.

How about removing each Anchovy?

3 That would make it less salty.

Let's remove them. What is the value of

```
remove_anchovy(
  Anchovy(
    Onion(
      Anchovy(
        Anchovy(
          Cheese(
            Crust))))))?
```

4 It should be a Cheese and Onion *pizza*, like this:

```
Onion(
  Cheese(
    Crust)).
```

What is the value of

```
remove_anchovy(
  Sausage(
    Onion(
      Anchovy(
        Sausage(
          Cheese(
            Crust))))))?
```

5 It should be a Cheese, Sausage, and Onion *pizza*, like this:

```
Sausage(
  Onion(
    Sausage(
      Cheese(
        Crust)))).
```

Does *remove_anchovy* consume *pizzas*?

6 Yes, and it produces them, too.

Fill in the blanks in the skeleton.

```
fun remove_anchovy(Crust)
    = Crust
  | remove_anchovy(Cheese(x))
    = ________
  | remove_anchovy(Onion(x))
    = ________
  | remove_anchovy(Anchovy(x))
    = ________
  | remove_anchovy(Sausage(x))
    = ________
```

```
remove_anchovy :
  pizza → pizza
```

7 We didn't expect you to know this one.

Fill in all the blanks except for the Anchovy line.

```
fun remove_anchovy(Crust)
    = Crust
  | remove_anchovy(Cheese(x))
    = Cheese(remove_anchovy(x))
  | remove_anchovy(Onion(x))
    = ________
  | remove_anchovy(Anchovy(x))
    = ________
  | remove_anchovy(Sausage(x))
    = ________
```

We've eaten the cheese already.

8 The Onion and Sausage lines are similar to the Cheese line.

```
fun remove_anchovy(Crust)
    = Crust
  | remove_anchovy(Cheese(x))
    = Cheese(remove_anchovy(x))
  | remove_anchovy(Onion(x))
    = Onion(remove_anchovy(x))
  | remove_anchovy(Anchovy(x))
    = ________
  | remove_anchovy(Sausage(x))
    = Sausage(remove_anchovy(x))
```

Explain why we use Cheese, Onion, and Sausage when we fill in the blanks.

9 For every Cheese, Onion, or Sausage that we see, we must put one back.

Since *remove_anchovy* must produce a *pizza*, let us use Crust, the simplest *pizza*, for the line that contains Anchovy(x).

```
fun remove_anchovy(Crust)
    = Crust
  | remove_anchovy(Cheese(x))
    = Cheese(remove_anchovy(x))
  | remove_anchovy(Onion(x))
    = Onion(remove_anchovy(x))
  | remove_anchovy(Anchovy(x))
    = Crust
  | remove_anchovy(Sausage(x))
    = Sausage(remove_anchovy(x))
```

10 Yes, *remove_anchovy* consumes *pizza* and produces *pizza* without Anchovy on it.

Let's try it out on a small pizza:

```
remove_anchovy(
  Anchovy(
    Crust)).
```

11 That's easy. It matches the Anchovy line, if x stands for Crust. And the answer is Crust.

Is

```
Crust
```

like

```
remove_anchovy(
  Anchovy(
    Crust))
```

without Anchovy?

12 Absolutely, but what if we had more anchovies?

No problem. Here is an example:

```
remove_anchovy(
  Anchovy(
    Anchovy(
      Crust))).
```

13 That's easy again. It also matches the Anchovy line and the answer is still Crust.

Okay, so what if we had onions on top:

```
remove_anchovy(
  Onion(
    Cheese(
      Anchovy(
        Anchovy(
          Crust)))))?
```

14 This matches

```
remove_anchovy(Onion(x))
```

if x stands for

```
Cheese(
  Anchovy(
    Anchovy(
      Crust))).
```

What is the value of

```
Onion(remove_anchovy(x))
```

if x stands for

```
Cheese(
  Anchovy(
    Anchovy(
      Crust)))?
```

15 It is the pizza that

```
remove_anchovy(
  Cheese(
    Anchovy(
      Anchovy(
        Crust))))
```

produces, with Onion added on top.

What is the value of

```
remove_anchovy(
  Cheese(
    Anchovy(
      Anchovy(
        Crust))))?
```

16 This matches

```
remove_anchovy(Cheese(x))
```

if x stands for

```
Anchovy(
  Anchovy(
    Crust)).
```

And what is the value of

```
Cheese(remove_anchovy(x))
```

if x stands for

```
Anchovy(
  Anchovy(
    Crust))?
```

17 It is the pizza that

```
remove_anchovy(
  Anchovy(
    Anchovy(
      Crust)))
```

produces, with Cheese added on top.

Do we know the value of

```
remove_anchovy(
  Anchovy(
    Anchovy(
      Crust)))?
```

18 Yes, we know that this produces Crust.

Does that mean that Crust is the answer?

19 No, we still have to add Cheese and Onion.

Does it matter in which order we add those two ingredients?

20 Yes, we must first add Cheese, producing

```
Cheese(
  Crust)
```

and then we add Onion.

So what is the final answer?

21 It is

```
Onion(
  Cheese(
    Crust)).
```

Can you describe in your own words what *remove_anchovy* does?

22 Here are our words:
"*remove_anchovy* looks at each topping of a *pizza* and makes a pizza with all the toppings that are above the first anchovy."

Is that what we wanted?

23 No. We wanted to keep all toppings except for anchovies.

Let's try one more example:

```
remove_anchovy(
  Cheese(
    Anchovy(
      Cheese(
        Crust)))).
```

What kind of pizza should this make?

24 It should be a double-cheese pizza.

Check it out!

25 It matches

remove_anchovy(Cheese(x))

if x stands for

```
Anchovy(
  Cheese(
    Crust)).
```

Doesn't that mean that the result is
Cheese(
  remove_anchovy(
    Anchovy(
      Cheese(
        Crust))))?

26 Yes, we have at least one Cheese topping.

What does
remove_anchovy(
  Anchovy(
    Cheese(
      Crust)))
match next?

27 This matches
remove_anchovy(Anchovy(x)).

And the answer is
Crust?

28 Yes, and just like before we need to add Cheese on top.

Does that mean the final answer is
Cheese(
  Crust)?

29 Yes, but that's not the answer we wanted.

What did we want?

30 A double-cheese pizza like
Cheese(
  Cheese(
    Crust)),
because that's what it means to remove anchovies and nothing else.

---

31 How do we have to change *remove_anchovy* to get the Cheese back?

The Anchovy line must produce *remove_anchovy*(*x*).

```
fun remove_anchovy(Crust)
    = Crust
  | remove_anchovy(Cheese(x))
    = Cheese(remove_anchovy(x))
  | remove_anchovy(Onion(x))
    = Onion(remove_anchovy(x))
  | remove_anchovy(Anchovy(x))
    = remove_anchovy(x)
  | remove_anchovy(Sausage(x))
    = Sausage(remove_anchovy(x))
```

---

32 Does this new version of *remove_anchovy* still consume *pizza*s?

Yes, and it still produces them.

---

33 You have earned yourself a double-cheese pizza.

And don't forget the anchovies.

---

34 Would you like even more cheese than that?

Some people like lots of cheese.

---

35 We could add cheese on top of the anchovies.

Yes, that would hide their taste a bit.

---

36 What kind of pizza is

```
top_anchovy_with_cheese(
  Onion(
    Anchovy(
      Cheese(
        Anchovy(
          Crust)))))?
```

Easy, there is a layer of Cheese on top of each Anchovy:

```
Onion(
  Cheese(
    Anchovy(
      Cheese(
        Cheese(
          Anchovy(
            Crust)))))).
```

37 And what is
top_anchovy_with_cheese(
Onion(
Cheese(
Sausage(
Crust))))?

Here we don't add any Cheese, because the pizza does not contain any Anchovy:
Onion(
Cheese(
Sausage(
Crust))).

38 Fill in the blanks in the skeleton.

```
fun top_anchovy_with_cheese(Crust)
      = Crust
  | top_anchovy_with_cheese(Cheese(x))
      = ________
  | top_anchovy_with_cheese(Onion(x))
      = ________
  | top_anchovy_with_cheese(Anchovy(x))
      = ________
  | top_anchovy_with_cheese(Sausage(x))
      = ________
```

```
top_anchovy_with_cheese :
  pizza → pizza
```
•

We expect you to know some of the answers.

```
fun top_anchovy_with_cheese(Crust)
      = Crust
  | top_anchovy_with_cheese(Cheese(x))
      = Cheese(top_anchovy_with_cheese(x))
  | top_anchovy_with_cheese(Onion(x))
      = Onion(top_anchovy_with_cheese(x))
  | top_anchovy_with_cheese(Anchovy(x))
      = ________
  | top_anchovy_with_cheese(Sausage(x))
      = Sausage(top_anchovy_with_cheese(x))
```

39 How does that skeleton compare with this one?

```
fun remove_anchovy(Crust)
      = Crust
  | remove_anchovy(Cheese(x))
      = Cheese(remove_anchovy(x))
  | remove_anchovy(Onion(x))
      = Onion(remove_anchovy(x))
  | remove_anchovy(Anchovy(x))
      = ________
  | remove_anchovy(Sausage(x))
      = Sausage(remove_anchovy(x))
```

The two skeletons are the same except for the names of the functions.

40 What function would we get if we filled the blank in the last skeleton for

top_anchovy_with_cheese

with

top_anchovy_with_cheese(x)?

We would get *remove_anchovy* but with a different name.

---

41 Then what do we have to put into the blank?

We must at least put the Anchovy back on the pizza.

---

42 And then?

We must top it with Cheese.

---

43 Let's do it!

Here it is.

```
fun top_anchovy_with_cheese(Crust)
    = Crust
  | top_anchovy_with_cheese(Cheese(x))
    = Cheese(top_anchovy_with_cheese(x))
  | top_anchovy_with_cheese(Onion(x))
    = Onion(top_anchovy_with_cheese(x))
  | top_anchovy_with_cheese(Anchovy(x))
    = Cheese(
        Anchovy(
          top_anchovy_with_cheese(x)))
  | top_anchovy_with_cheese(Sausage(x))
    = Sausage(top_anchovy_with_cheese(x))
```

---

44 What type of value does

top_anchovy_with_cheese

produce?

The difference between

top_anchovy_with_cheese

and

remove_anchovy

is one line. Cheese on top of Anchovy on a pizza still makes *pizza*, so the type of

top_anchovy_with_cheese

is

pizza $\rightarrow$ *pizza*.

45 How many occurrences of Cheese are in the result of

```
top_anchovy_with_cheese(
  remove_anchovy(
    Onion(
      Anchovy(
        Cheese(
          Anchovy(
            Crust))))))?
```

One, because *remove_anchovy* removes all anchovies, so that *top_anchovy_with_cheese* doesn't add any cheese.

46 How many occurrences of Cheese are in the result of

```
remove_anchovy(
  top_anchovy_with_cheese(
    Onion(
      Anchovy(
        Cheese(
          Anchovy(
            Crust))))))?
```

Three, because *top_anchovy_with_cheese* first adds Cheese for each Anchovy. Then *remove_anchovy* removes all anchovies:

```
Onion(
  Cheese(
    Cheese(
      Cheese(
        Crust)))).
```

47 Perhaps we should replace every Anchovy with Cheese.

We just did that for one pizza.

48 Is it true that for each Anchovy in x

```
remove_anchovy(
  top_anchovy_with_cheese(x))
```

adds some Cheese as long as x is a pizza?

Yes, and it does more. Once all the cheese is added, the anchovies are removed.

49 So is this the correct definition of *subst_anchovy_by_cheese*?

```
fun subst_anchovy_by_cheese(x)
    = remove_anchovy(
        top_anchovy_with_cheese(x))
```

```
subst_anchovy_by_cheese :
  pizza → pizza
```

Yes, it is. This function replaces each instance of Anchovy by Cheese.

50 Can you describe in your own words how

subst_anchovy_by_cheese

works?

Here are our words:

"*subst_anchovy_by_cheese* looks at each topping of a pizza and adds Cheese on top of each Anchovy. Then, it looks at each topping again, including all the new cheese, and removes the anchovies."

---

51 Here are some different words:

"*subst_anchovy_by_cheese* looks at each topping of a pizza and replaces each Anchovy by Cheese."

Can you define a function that matches this description and doesn't use *remove_anchovy* and *top_anchovy_with_cheese*?

Yes, here is a skeleton.

```
fun subst_anchovy_by_cheese(Crust)
    = Crust
  | subst_anchovy_by_cheese(Cheese(x))
    = Cheese(subst_anchovy_by_cheese(x))
  | subst_anchovy_by_cheese(Onion(x))
    = Onion(subst_anchovy_by_cheese(x))
  | subst_anchovy_by_cheese(Anchovy(x))
    = __________
  | subst_anchovy_by_cheese(Sausage(x))
    = Sausage(subst_anchovy_by_cheese(x))
```

---

52 Does this skeleton look familiar?

Yes, this skeleton looks just like those of

top_anchovy_with_cheese

and

remove_anchovy.

---

53 Fill in the blank.

```
fun subst_anchovy_by_cheese(Crust)
    = Crust
  | subst_anchovy_by_cheese(Cheese(x))
    = Cheese(subst_anchovy_by_cheese(x))
  | subst_anchovy_by_cheese(Onion(x))
    = Onion(subst_anchovy_by_cheese(x))
  | subst_anchovy_by_cheese(Anchovy(x))
    = __________
  | subst_anchovy_by_cheese(Sausage(x))
    = Sausage(subst_anchovy_by_cheese(x))
```

Here it is.

```
fun subst_anchovy_by_cheese(Crust)
    = Crust
  | subst_anchovy_by_cheese(Cheese(x))
    = Cheese(subst_anchovy_by_cheese(x))
  | subst_anchovy_by_cheese(Onion(x))
    = Onion(subst_anchovy_by_cheese(x))
  | subst_anchovy_by_cheese(Anchovy(x))
    = Cheese(subst_anchovy_by_cheese(x))
  | subst_anchovy_by_cheese(Sausage(x))
    = Sausage(subst_anchovy_by_cheese(x))
```

Now you can replace Anchovy with whatever *pizza* topping you want.	[54] We will stick with anchovies.

The Third Moral

Functions that produce values of a datatype must use the associated constructors to build data of that type.

4.
Look to the Stars

Are you tired of making pizza?

1 We are too. Let's make complete meals.

Do you like shrimp cocktail?

2 We do, too.

We like Hummus for meza too.

3 And how about some Escargots?

Okay, let's sum them up.

```
datatype meza =
   Shrimp
 | Calamari
 | Escargots
 | Hummus
```

4 There is a new one, too: Calamari.

And here are some entrées.

```
datatype main =
   Steak
 | Ravioli
 | Chicken
 | Eggplant
```

5 We should also have some salads.

```
datatype salad =
   Green
 | Cucumber
 | Greek
```

Let's not forget the fun part.

6 Yes, we need desserts.

```
datatype dessert =
   Sundae
 | Mousse
 | Torte
```

Now let's make a meal.

7 Don't we have to put together different courses when we make full meals?

No, we can use stars!

8 What is a star?

Here is our first three star meal:
(Calamari,Ravioli,Greek,Sundae).

9 It looks like a meal.

How many items does this meal have?

10 Four, and they are separated by commas and enclosed in parentheses.

Is
(Hummus,Steak,Green,Torte)
a meal of the same type?

11 Yes, it also consists of four items in the same order: *meza*, *main*, *salad*, and *dessert*.

Does
(Torte,Hummus,Steak,Sundae)
belong to the same type?

12 We have seen meals like this before, but *dessert* should never be the first course.

The first kind of meal is of type
$(\mathit{meza} * \mathit{main} * \mathit{salad} * \mathit{dessert})$.

13 Does this mean that the type of the thing that is not a meal is
$(\mathit{dessert} * \mathit{meza} * \mathit{main} * \mathit{dessert})$?

What's unusual about our meals?

14 People here eat the salads before the main course:
$(\mathit{meza} * \mathit{salad} * \mathit{main} * \mathit{dessert})$.

Is that a meal?

15 It is not the same kind of meal, is it?

No, it is not. Each star corresponds to a comma in the construction of a meal.

16 And the order matters, right?

Yes, the order matters, but do we have to have three stars in meals?

17 No, if we want small meals with three courses, we only need two stars. And if we want tiny meals with two courses, we need only one.

What is your favorite kind of meal with only two ingredients?

18 Ours is

(Shrimp,Sundae).

What is the type of that tiny meal?

19 (*meza* $*$ *dessert*).

Have you tasted your sundae yet?

20 We just ate ours.

What is

add_a_steak(Shrimp)?

21 It is a tiny meal:

(Shrimp,Steak).

What is

add_a_steak(Hummus)?

22 This meal needs something to sink our teeth into.

(Hummus,Steak).

Does *add_a_steak* consume *meza*?

23 Yes, it does.

Does *add_a_steak* produce a tiny meal?

24 Yes, this function always produces a tiny meal. Indeed, we even know that the second item is always Steak.

Is this a definition of *add_a_steak*?

```
fun add_a_steak(Shrimp)
      = (Shrimp,Steak)
  | add_a_steak(Calamari)
      = (Calamari,Steak)
  | add_a_steak(Escargots)
      = (Escargots,Steak)
  | add_a_steak(Hummus)
      = (Hummus,Steak)
```

What is its type?

25 It is a function and we already discussed what it consumes and produces.

```
add_a_steak :
  meza → (meza * main)
```

Isn't this long for something so simple?

26 Yes, four lines is a lot. Can we shorten it?

It doesn't really matter what the *meza* is, so we can just give it a name in the pattern and use that name in the answer. Define the abridged version of *add_a_steak*.

27 With this hint, it is a piece of cake (which, by the way, isn't a *dessert*).

```
fun add_a_steak(x)
    = (x,Steak)
```

What is the value of *add_a_steak*(Escargots)?

28 (Escargots,Steak).

And how about *add_a_steak*(5)?

29 Isn't this nonsense?

It should be.

30 But is it?

It would be nonsense had we only used the first version of *add_a_steak*.

31 Correct. It consumed only *meza*.

What does the abridged version of *add_a_steak* consume?

32 Anything.

So what is its type?

33 We have always used α when a function could consume anything.

add_a_steak :
$\alpha \rightarrow (\alpha * main)$

Does that mean the second version of *add_a_steak* is more general than the first?

34 Yes, the second version exists for many different types. Therefore it can consume *mezas*, or *desserts*, or *nums*, and even *mains*.

Are both definitions correct?

35 Yes, they both add a Steak.

Why should we choose one over the other?

36 We know that the second one is more general, but it is also always one line long. The first kind of definition always contains as many lines as there are alternatives in the **datatype** definition.

Is it always better to use the more general version?

37 No, the more specific one is more accurate, so using it will reveal nonsense more often.

Could we have used this idea of shortening functions before?

38 Yes, we should have known about this shorthand when we defined *remove_anchovy*. It could have been so much shorter.

```
fun remove_anchovy(Crust)
    = Crust
  | remove_anchovy(Anchovy(x))
    = remove_anchovy(x)
  | remove_anchovy(C(x))
    = C(remove_anchovy(x))
```

⊗

Nice dream, but it is impossible for a variable like C to stand in place of a constructor that consumes values as we did in the third line.

39 Too bad.

Here is a lollypop.

40 That helps a little.

Let's write the function *eq_main*, which takes two *main* dishes and determines whether they are the same.

41 Does that mean we need to compare all four possible *main* dishes with each other?

Yes, that is precisely what we mean.

42 Here it is.

```
fun eq_main(Steak,Steak)
      = true
  | eq_main(Steak,Ravioli)
      = false
  | eq_main(Steak,Chicken)
      = false
  | eq_main(Steak,Eggplant)
      = false
  | eq_main(Ravioli,Steak)
      = false
  | eq_main(Ravioli,Ravioli)
      = true
  | eq_main(Ravioli,Chicken)
      = false
  | eq_main(Ravioli,Eggplant)
      = false
  | eq_main(Chicken,Steak)
      = false
  | eq_main(Chicken,Ravioli)
      = false
  | eq_main(Chicken,Chicken)
      = true
  | eq_main(Chicken,Eggplant)
      = false
  | eq_main(Eggplant,Steak)
      = false
  | eq_main(Eggplant,Ravioli)
      = false
  | eq_main(Eggplant,Chicken)
      = false
  | eq_main(Eggplant,Eggplant)
      = true
```

Where is its type?

43 Here.

```
eq_main :
  (main * main) → bool
```

•

44 How does this type differ from the type of *add_a_steak*?

It has a star to the left of → instead of the right.

45 Does that mean *eq_main* consumes two things?

Not really, it consumes a pair of *main* dishes, which we sometimes think of as two dishes.

46 Here is a shorter version.

```
fun eq_main(Steak,Steak)
      = true
  | eq_main(Ravioli,Ravioli)
      = true
  | eq_main(Chicken,Chicken)
      = true
  | eq_main(Eggplant,Eggplant)
      = true
  | eq_main(a_main,another_main)
      = false
```

This is much shorter than the previous one and it contains far fewer patterns

47 Yes, once we have defined a function, we may be able to rearrange patterns and make a function shorter.

That's neat but who could have figured that out?

48 What is the value of
has_steak(Hummus,Ravioli,Sundae)?

false.

49 And
has_steak(Shrimp,Steak,Mousse)?

true.

50 Good. What does the function consume?

A small meal consisting of *meza*, *main*, and *dessert*.

51 What does it produce?

bool.

What is the type of *has_steak*?

52 (*meza* $*$ *main* $*$ *dessert*) $\rightarrow$ *bool*.

Could we write the unabridged version of *has_steak*?

53 It would make our fingers too tired.

Let's define just the abridged version of *has_steak*.

54 That's easy.

```
fun has_steak(a_meza,Steak,a_dessert)
    = true
  | has_steak(a_meza,a_main,a_dessert)
    = false
```

What is its type?

55 It does consume *meza*, a *main* dish, and a *dessert*. So, it seems that this is the type:

(*meza* $*$ *main* $*$ *dessert*) $\rightarrow$ *bool*.

That's true. But is

has_steak(5,Steak,true)

nonsense?

56 Nearly. If *has_steak* has the type we said it has, then it is nonsense.

So, is it nonsense?

57 The definition of *has_steak* does not prevent it from consuming 5 and true.

Then what is the type of this abridged version of *has_steak*?

58 We need another Greek letter like α to make the type.

Why?

59 Because the first and the third components do not need to belong to the same type. Therefore we must say the third component is arbitrary, yet differs from the first.

Here is the type.

has_steak :
$(\alpha * main * \beta$[1]$) \to bool$ •

[1] We use 'b for β, but it is pronounced beta.

60 Good, but could we also have written this?

has_steak :
$(\beta * main * \alpha) \to bool$ •

Yes, the two types are identical except for the Greek names of the types.

61 They both say that *has_steak* consumes three things, the first and third belong to arbitrary, distinct types.

Do α and β always stand for different types?

62 No, *has_steak* can also consume (5,Ravioli,6).

We won't use any other Greek letters,

63 That's good.

Does it make sense to have *has_steak* consume (5,Ravioli,6)?

64 No, *has_steak* should consume only *meza* and *dessert*s along with a *main* dish.

Is it possible to restrict the function so that it would consume only good things?

65 We could say its type is this.

has_steak :
$(meza * main * dessert) \to bool$ •

Unfortunately, that is only enough for us because we agreed to respect these statements about the types of functions. If we really want to restrict the type of things *has_steak* consumes, we need to combine the bulleted type boxes with the definitions.

```
fun has_steak(a:meza,Steak,d:dessert):bool
    = true
  | has_steak(a:meza,ns,d:dessert):bool
    = false
```

66 Looks simple. It is obvious where the various underlined pieces come from.

67 If it looks simple, why not combine the type of the first version of *add_a_steak* and the second definition to restrict its use, too.

```
fun add_a_steak(x)
  = (x,Steak)
```

```
add_a_steak :
  meza → (meza * main)
```

•

Here it is:

```
fun add_a_steak(x:meza):(meza * main)
  = (x,Steak)
```

68 Relax and enjoy a hot fudge sundae.

After a delicious Turkish meza platter.

The Fourth Moral

Some functions consume values of star type; some produce values of star type.

5.
Couples Are Magnificent, Too

Have we seen this kind of definition before?

```
datatype α pizza =
   Bottom
 | Topping of (α * (α pizza))
```

1 What? More pizza!

Yes, still more pizza, but this one is interesting.

2 Yes, we have seen something like this kind of definition before. A type definition using α abbreviates many different type definitions. But isn't this the first **datatype** definition that uses a star?

Yes, it is. Use a **datatype** definition to describe the shape that is like the type *fish pizza* using this definition of *fish*.

```
datatype fish =
   Anchovy
 | Lox
 | Tuna
```

3 Here it is.[1]

```
datatype fish pizza =
   Bottom
 | Topping of (fish * (fish pizza))                ⊗
```

[1] Recall that ⊗ indicates that this definition is ungrammatical, but this definition expresses the idea best.

Is

```
Topping(Anchovy,
  Topping(Tuna,
    Topping(Anchovy,
      Bottom)))
```

a pizza of type *fish pizza*?

4 It is a *fish pizza* provided

```
Topping(Tuna,
  Topping(Anchovy,
    Bottom))
```

is a *fish pizza*, because Topping makes these kinds of pizzas.

Is

```
Topping(Tuna,
  Topping(Anchovy,
    Bottom))
```

a *fish pizza*?

5 Yes, it too is a *fish pizza*, if

```
Topping(Anchovy,
  Bottom)
```

is a *fish pizza*.

6 Is
Topping(Anchovy,
 Bottom)
a *fish pizza*?

Yes, it is, because Topping constructs a *fish pizza* from Anchovy—a fish—and Bottom—a *fish pizza*.

---

7 Is Bottom really a *fish pizza*?

Yes, because Bottom is at the bottom of many kinds of pizzas. We could also put it at the bottom of an *int pizza*, a *bool pizza*, or a *num pizza*.

---

8 What is the value of

```
rem_anchovy(
  Topping(Lox,
    Topping(Anchovy,
      Topping(Tuna,
        Topping(Anchovy,
          Bottom)))))?
```

It is this *fish pizza*:

```
Topping(Lox,
  Topping(Tuna,
    Bottom)).
```

---

9 Is it true that the value of

```
rem_anchovy(
  Topping(Lox,
    Topping(Tuna,
      Bottom)))
```

is

```
Topping(Lox,
  Topping(Tuna,
    Bottom))?
```

Yes, the pizza that comes out is the same as the one that goes in.

---

10 Does *rem_anchovy* consume *fish pizza* and produce *fish pizza*?

Yes, it does, and it does not consume a *num pizza* or an *int pizza*.

Define *rem_anchovy*. Here is a skeleton.

```
fun rem_anchovy(Bottom)
    = __________
  | rem_anchovy(Topping(Anchovy,p))
    = __________
  | rem_anchovy(Topping(Tuna,p))
    = __________
  | rem_anchovy(Topping(Lox,p))
    = __________
```

rem_anchovy **:**
(*fish pizza*) → (*fish pizza*) •

11 This is easy by now.

```
fun rem_anchovy(Bottom)
    = Bottom
  | rem_anchovy(Topping(Anchovy,p))
    = rem_anchovy(p)
  | rem_anchovy(Topping(Tuna,p))
    = Topping(Tuna,rem_anchovy(p))
  | rem_anchovy(Topping(Lox,p))
    = Topping(Lox,rem_anchovy(p))
```

Is there a shorter version of *rem_anchovy*?

12 Yes, we can combine the last two patterns and their answers if we let t stand for either Tuna or Lox.

Do we expect you to know that?

13 No, but here is the definition.

```
fun rem_anchovy(Bottom)
    = Bottom
  | rem_anchovy(Topping(Anchovy,p))
    = rem_anchovy(p)
  | rem_anchovy(Topping(t,p))
    = Topping(t,rem_anchovy(p))
```

How does
rem_tuna
differ from
rem_anchovy?

14 Not much. It removes Tuna instead of Anchovy. Here is the definition.

```
fun rem_tuna(Bottom)
    = Bottom
  | rem_tuna(Topping(Anchovy,p))
    = Topping(Anchovy,rem_tuna(p))
  | rem_tuna(Topping(Tuna,p))
    = rem_tuna(p)
  | rem_tuna(Topping(Lox,p))
    = Topping(Lox,rem_tuna(p))
```

Where is the type?

15 Here it is.

```
rem_tuna :
  (fish pizza) → (fish pizza)
```

Can we shorten this definition like we shortened that of *rem_anchovy*?

16 No, the patterns and answers that are alike are too far apart.

How do the following two definitions of *fish* differ?

```
datatype fish =
   Anchovy
 | Lox
 | Tuna
```

```
datatype fish =
   Tuna
 | Lox
 | Anchovy
```

17 They aren't really different, because they both say that Lox, Anchovy, and Tuna are *fish*. But, if we had chosen the second definition, we would have defined *rem_tuna* like this.

```
fun rem_tuna(Bottom)
      = Bottom
  | rem_tuna(Topping(Tuna,p))
      = rem_tuna(p)
  | rem_tuna(Topping(Lox,p))
      = Topping(Lox,rem_tuna(p))
  | rem_tuna(Topping(Anchovy,p))
      = Topping(Anchovy,rem_tuna(p))
```

```
rem_tuna :
  (fish pizza) → (fish pizza)
```

Why would we have defined *rem_tuna* like that?

18 Because we have always ordered the patterns according to the alternatives in the corresponding **datatype** definition.

Can we shorten this new definition of *rem_tuna*?

19 Yes, because the pair of patterns and answers that are alike are close together.

Do we have to change the definition of *fish* to do all that?

20 No, we don't. The ordering of the patterns does not matter as long as there is one for each alternative in the corresponding **datatype** definition. But we like to keep things in the same order.

Write a shorter version of *rem_tuna*.

```
fun rem_tuna(Bottom)
    = Bottom
  | rem_tuna(Topping(Tuna,p))
    = rem_tuna(p)
  | rem_tuna(Topping(Lox,p))
    = Topping(Lox,rem_tuna(p))
  | rem_tuna(Topping(Anchovy,p))
    = Topping(Anchovy,rem_tuna(p))
```

21 Here's one.

```
fun rem_tuna(Bottom)
    = Bottom
  | rem_tuna(Topping(Tuna,p))
    = rem_tuna(p)
  | rem_tuna(Topping(t,p))
    = Topping(t,rem_tuna(p))
```

Can we combine *rem_anchovy* and *rem_tuna* into one function?

22 Yes, but when we use the combined function, we need to say which kind of fish we want to remove.

What is a good name for the combined function?

23 How about *rem_fish*?

How do we use *rem_fish*?

24 We give it a pair of things. The first component could be the kind of fish we want to remove and the second one could be the pizza.

Could we also give it a pair where the second component is the kind of fish we want to remove and the first one is the pizza?

25 Yes, it doesn't matter as long as we stick to one choice.

What would be the type of *rem_fish* if we chose the second alternative?

26 That's easy:

$$((\textit{fish pizza}) * \textit{fish}) \rightarrow (\textit{fish pizza}).$$

But, let's use the first one.

27 Then *rem_fish* consumes a pair that consists of a *fish* and a *fish pizza*.

Here is the definition of *rem_fish*.

```
fun rem_fish(x,Bottom)
      = Bottom
  | rem_fish(Tuna,Topping(Tuna,p))
      = rem_fish(Tuna,p)
  | rem_fish(Tuna,Topping(t,p))
      = Topping(t,rem_fish(Tuna,p))
  | rem_fish(Anchovy,Topping(Anchovy,p))
      = rem_fish(Anchovy,p)
  | rem_fish(Anchovy,Topping(t,p))
      = Topping(t,rem_fish(Anchovy,p))
  | rem_fish(Lox,Topping(Lox,p))
      = rem_fish(Lox,p)
  | rem_fish(Lox,Topping(t,p))
      = Topping(t,rem_fish(Lox,p))
```

```
rem_fish :
  (fish * (fish pizza)) → (fish pizza)
```

Isn't this clumsy?

28 As we will see, it could have been worse.

Describe in your words how it could have been worse.

29 Here are ours:
"The pattern

rem_fish(Tuna,Topping(t,p))

matches all pairs that consist of Tuna and a *fish pizza* whose topping is not Tuna. For the long version of *rem_fish* we would have used two different patterns:

rem_fish(Tuna,Topping(Anchovy,p))

and

rem_fish(Tuna,Topping(Lox,p)).

And, we would also have needed an answer for each pattern."

Write the unabridged version of *rem_fish*.

30 It has three more patterns than the short one.

```
fun rem_fish(x,Bottom)
      = Bottom
  | rem_fish(Tuna,Topping(Tuna,p))
      = rem_fish(Tuna,p)
  | rem_fish(Tuna,Topping(Anchovy,p))
      = Topping(Anchovy,rem_fish(Tuna,p))
  | rem_fish(Tuna,Topping(Lox,p))
      = Topping(Lox,rem_fish(Tuna,p))
  | rem_fish(Anchovy,Topping(Anchovy,p))
      = rem_fish(Anchovy,p)
  | rem_fish(Anchovy,Topping(Lox,p))
      = Topping(Lox,rem_fish(Anchovy,p))
  | rem_fish(Anchovy,Topping(Tuna,p))
      = Topping(Tuna,rem_fish(Anchovy,p))
  | rem_fish(Lox,Topping(Lox,p))
      = rem_fish(Lox,p)
  | rem_fish(Lox,Topping(Anchovy,p))
      = Topping(Anchovy,rem_fish(Lox,p))
  | rem_fish(Lox,Topping(Tuna,p))
      = Topping(Tuna,rem_fish(Lox,p))
```

If we add another kind of fish to our **datatype**, what happens to the short function?

31 We have to add two patterns and two answers.

If we add another kind of fish to our **datatype**, what happens to the unabridged version?

32 We have to add one pattern and one answer for each old kind of fish and four patterns and answers for the new kind.

Why does the unabridged version get so large?

33 Because we must compare each kind of fish to every other kind of fish, including itself. And the first pattern is always a test for Bottom.

Does that mean the unabridged version for five fish contains 26 patterns?

34 Yes, and for six fish it would be 37. Worse, if n is the number of fish in a **datatype**, the number of patterns needed for the unabridged version is $n^2 + 1$.

35 Is there a shorter way to determine whether two fish are the same?

Could we use the same name in one pattern twice?

```
fun rem_fish(x,Bottom)
    = Bottom
  | rem_fish(x,Topping(x,p))
    = rem_fish(x,p)
  | rem_fish(x,Topping(t,p))
    = Topping(t,rem_fish(x,p))
```

⊗

36 Wouldn't that be great? Unfortunately, using the same name *twice* in a pattern is ungrammatical.

Sigh.

37 Let's define the function *eq_fish*, which determines whether two given *fish* are equal.

That function consumes a pair of *fish* and produces a *bool*.

38 The unabridged version of *eq_fish* is huge.

```
fun eq_fish(Anchovy,Anchovy)
    = true
  | eq_fish(Anchovy,Lox)
    = false
  | eq_fish(Anchovy,Tuna)
    = false
  | eq_fish(Lox,Anchovy)
    = false
  | eq_fish(Lox,Lox)
    = true
  | eq_fish(Lox,Tuna)
    = false
  | eq_fish(Tuna,Anchovy)
    = false
  | eq_fish(Tuna,Lox)
    = false
  | eq_fish(Tuna,Tuna)
    = true
```

Write the abridged version and provide a type?

It is only four lines long.

```
fun eq_fish(Anchovy,Anchovy)
    = true
  | eq_fish(Lox,Lox)
    = true
  | eq_fish(Tuna,Tuna)
    = true
  | eq_fish(a_fish,another_fish)
    = false
```

```
eq_fish :
  (fish * fish) → bool
```

•

What is the value of
eq_fish(Anchovy,Anchovy)?

39 It is true, unlike *eq_fish*(Anchovy,Tuna).

Here is the shortest version of *rem_fish* yet.

```
fun rem_fish(x,Bottom)
    = Bottom
  | rem_fish(x,Topping(t,p))
    = if eq_fish(t,x)
        then rem_fish(x,p)
        else Topping(t,(rem_fish(x,p)))
```

Is there anything new?

40 Yes, it contains

if exp_1
then exp_2
else exp_3,

which we haven't seen before. How do we determine its type?

To determine its type, we first make sure that the type of exp_1 is *bool*, and then we determine the types of exp_2 and exp_3.

41 And these two need to be the same because the value of either one can be the result of the entire expression. Correct?

Yes, great guess. Does this version of *rem_fish* still have the type
(*fish* ∗ (*fish pizza*)) → (*fish pizza*)?

42 Yes, since both *rem_fish* and Topping produce *fish pizza*, *rem_fish* produces *fish pizza*, no matter which of exp_2 or exp_3 is evaluated.

How does that new version differ from this ungrammatical one?

```
fun rem_fish(x,Bottom)
    = Bottom
  | rem_fish(x,Topping(x,p))
    = rem_fish(x,p)
  | rem_fish(x,Topping(t,p))
    = Topping(t,rem_fish(x,p))
                                    ⊗
```

43 Not too much. The shortest version uses *eq_fish* to compare the two kinds of fish; this one uses an ungrammatical pattern.

Let's try it out with the shortest version:
rem_fish(Anchovy,
  Topping(Anchovy,
    Bottom)).

44 It does not match the first pattern, because the pizza is not Bottom.

Does the second pattern match?	45 If x is Anchovy, t is Anchovy, and p is Bottom, then it matches.
What next?	46 Next we need to compare t with x, which are equal, so *eq_fish*(t,x) is true.
Therefore, we take *rem_fish*(x,p) as the answer.	47 Since p is Bottom, the result of that expression is Bottom, and that is also the result of *rem_fish*(Anchovy, Topping(Anchovy, Bottom)).
What is the value of *rem_fish*(Tuna, Topping(Anchovy, Topping(Tuna, Topping(Anchovy, Bottom))))?	48 Again, the first pattern doesn't match, but the other one does, if x is Tuna, t is Anchovy, and p is Topping(Tuna, Topping(Anchovy, Bottom)).
What is *eq_fish*(t,x) if t is Anchovy and x is Tuna?	49 false.
So what is the answer?	50 The answer is Topping(Anchovy, *rem_fish*(Tuna, Topping(Tuna, Topping(Anchovy, Bottom)))), which is what follows the pattern and the = sign with x replaced by Tuna, t replaced by Anchovy, and p replaced by Topping(Tuna, Topping(Anchovy, Bottom)).

Which pattern does
rem_fish(Tuna,
  Topping(Tuna,
    Topping(Anchovy,
      Bottom)))
match?

51 It matches the second one again if x is Tuna, t is Tuna, and p is
  Topping(Anchovy,
    Bottom).

And how do we continue?

52 We determine the value of
rem_fish(Tuna,
  Topping(Anchovy,
    Bottom)),
because we want to remove Tuna.

Is
  Topping(Anchovy,
    Bottom)
the value of
rem_fish(Tuna,
  Topping(Anchovy,
    Bottom))?

53 Yes, because the pizza does not contain any Tuna.

So what is the final answer?

54 We still need to top it with anchovy:
  Topping(Anchovy,
    Topping(Anchovy,
      Bottom)).

Does
rem_int(3,
  Topping(2,
    Topping(3,
      Topping(2,
        Bottom))))
look familiar?

55 Yes, it looks like what we just evaluated.

What does *rem_int* do?

56 It removes *ints* from *int pizzas* just as *rem_fish* removes *fish* from *fish pizzas*.

With *eq_int*,[1] define *rem_int*.

57 That's easy, it is nearly identical to the definition of *rem_fish*.

```
fun rem_int(x,Bottom)
      = Bottom
   | rem_int(x,Topping(t,p))
      = if eq_int(t,x)
          then rem_int(x,p)
          else Topping(t,(rem_int(x,p)))
```

```
rem_int :
  (int * (int pizza)) → (int pizza)
```

[1] You must define `eq_int` as `fun eq_int(n:int,m:int) = (n = m).`

Describe how *rem_fish* differs from *rem_int*.

58 Here is what is on our mind:
"They look alike, but they differ in the types of the things that they consume and produce, and therefore in how they compare toppings.

Can we define one function that removes toppings from many kinds of pizza?

59 Yes, but not until chapter 8.

What is the value of
subst_fish(Lox,Anchovy,
 Topping(Anchovy,
  Topping(Tuna,
   Topping(Anchovy,
    Bottom))))?

60 It is the same pizza with all instances of Anchovy replaced by Lox:
Topping(Lox,
 Topping(Tuna,
  Topping(Lox,
   Bottom))).

What value does *subst_fish* consume?

61 It consumes a triple whose first two components are of type *fish* and whose last component is a *fish pizza*.

And what does it produce?

62 It always produces a *fish pizza*.

What is the value of
subst_int(5,3,
Topping(3,
Topping(2,
Topping(3,
Bottom))))?

63 It is the same pizza with all 3s replaced by 5s:
Topping(5,
Topping(2,
Topping(5,
Bottom))).

What value does *subst_int* consume?

64 It consumes a triple whose first two components are of type *int* and whose last component is an *int pizza*.

And what does it produce?

65 It always produces an *int pizza*.

We can define *subst_fish*.

```
fun subst_fish(n,a,Bottom)
    = Bottom
  | subst_fish(n,a,Topping(t,p))
    = if eq_fish(t,a)
        then Topping(n,subst_fish(n,a,p))
        else Topping(t,subst_fish(n,a,p))
```

```
subst_fish :
  (fish * fish * (fish pizza)) → (fish pizza)
```

Can we define *subst_int*?

66 To get from *subst_fish* to *subst_int*, we just need to substitute *fish* by *int* everywhere.

```
fun subst_int(n,a,Bottom)
    = Bottom
  | subst_int(n,a,Topping(t,p))
    = if eq_int(t,a)
        then Topping(n,subst_int(n,a,p))
        else Topping(t,subst_int(n,a,p))
```

```
subst_int :
  (int * int * (int pizza)) → (int pizza)
```

---

eq_int(17,0)?

67 false,
because 17 and 0 are different.

---

eq_int(17,Tuna)?

68 This is nonsense,[1] because 17 and Tuna belong to two different types.

[1] Remember that we use the word "nonsense" to refer to expressions that have no type.

What is the value of
eq_num(
  One_more_than(
    Zero),
  One_more_than(
    Zero))?

69 true,
because both values are constructed with One_more_than and the same component.

Define *eq_num*, but don't forget that it takes two values.

70 It is easy to write the unabridged version if we use two patterns for each value that it consumes.

```
fun eq_num(Zero,Zero)
      = true
   | eq_num(One_more_than(n),Zero)
      = false
   | eq_num(Zero,One_more_than(m))
      = false
   | eq_num(
        One_more_than(n),
        One_more_than(m))
      = eq_num(n,m)
```

Define the abridged version. Here is a version where we reordered some patterns. Can the last two be combined?

```
fun eq_num(Zero,Zero)
      = true
   | eq_num(
        One_more_than(n),
        One_more_than(m))
      = eq_num(n,m)
   | eq_num(One_more_than(n),Zero)
      = false
   | eq_num(Zero,One_more_than(m))
      = false
```

71 No problem.

```
fun eq_num(Zero,Zero)
      = true
   | eq_num(
        One_more_than(n),
        One_more_than(m))
      = eq_num(n,m)
   | eq_num(n,m)
      = false
```

No problem?

72 Not if we start from a correct program and carefully transform it, step by step.

Perhaps it is time to digest something besides this book.	73	Great idea. How about a granola bar and a walk?

The Fifth Moral

Write the first draft of a function following all the morals. When it is correct and no sooner, simplify.

6.
Oh My, It's Full of Stars!

Is

```
Flat(Apple,
  Flat(Peach,
    Bud))
```

a flat *tree*?

1 Yes.

Is

```
Flat(Pear,
  Bud)
```

a flat *tree*?

2 Yes, it is also a flat *tree*.

And how about

```
Split(
  Bud,
  Flat(Fig,
    Split(
      Bud,
      Bud)))?
```

3 No, it contains Split, so it can't be flat.

Here is one more example:

```
Split(
  Split(
    Bud,
    Flat(Lemon,
      Bud)),
  Flat(Fig,
    Split(
      Bud,
      Bud))).
```

Is it flat?

4 No, it isn't flat either.

Ready to go?

5 Sure. Let's define the **datatypes** we need to make this work.

Here are some fruits.

```
datatype fruit =
   Peach
 | Apple
 | Pear
 | Lemon
 | Fig
```

Let's say all *trees* are either flat, split, or bud. Formulate the **datatype** for *trees*.

6 It does not differ too much from the **datatypes** we have seen before.

```
datatype tree =
   Bud
 | Flat of fruit * tree
 | Split of tree * tree
```

How is it different from all the other **datatypes** we have seen before?

7 The name of the new **datatype** occurs twice in one (the last) alternative.

How many patterns does the definition of *flat_only* contain?

8 Three, because it consumes *trees*, and the **datatype** *tree* contains three alternatives.

What type of value does *flat_only* produce?

9 *bool*.

What function does *flat_only* remind us of?

10 *only_onions*.

Here is a skeleton for *flat_only*.

```
fun flat_only(Bud)
    = ________
  | flat_only(Flat(f,t))
    = ________
  | flat_only(Split(s,t))
    = ________
```

Fill in the blanks and supply the type.

11 That's easy now.

```
fun flat_only(Bud)
    = true
  | flat_only(Flat(f,t))
    = flat_only(t)
  | flat_only(Split(s,t))
    = false
```

```
flat_only :
  tree → bool
```

Define the function *split_only*, which checks whether a tree is constructed with Split and Bud only.

12 Here is the easy part.

```
fun split_only(Bud)
    = true
  | split_only(Flat(f,t))
    = false
  | split_only(Split(s,t))
    = ________
```

What is difficult about the last line?

13 We need to check whether both s and t are split trees.

Isn't that easy?

14 Yes, we just use *split_only* on s and t.

And then?

15 Then we need to know that both are true.

Doesn't that mean we need to know that *split_only*(t) is true if *split_only*(s) is true?

16 Yes.

Do we need to know whether *split_only*(t) is true if *split_only*(s) is false?

17 No, then the answer is false.

Finish the definition of *split_only* using
if ...
then ...
else ... .

18 Now we can do it.

```
fun split_only(Bud)
    = true
  | split_only(Flat(f,t))
    = false
  | split_only(Split(s,t))
    = if[1] split_only(s)
        then split_only(t)
        else false
```

```
split_only :
  tree → bool
```

[1] We could have written this **if**-expression as `split_only(s) andalso split_only(t)`.

Give an example of a *tree* for which *split_only* responds with true.

19 There is a trivial one: Bud.

How about one with five uses of Split?

20 Here is one:

```
Split(
  Split(
    Bud,
    Split(
      Bud,
      Bud)),
  Split(
    Bud,
    Split(
      Bud,
      Bud))).
```

Does this *tree* contain any fruit?

21 No tree for which *split_only* is true contains any fruit.

Here is one version of the definition of the function *contains_fruit*.

```
fun contains_fruit(Bud)
    = false
  | contains_fruit(Flat(f,t))
    = true
  | contains_fruit(Split(s,t))
    = if¹ contains_fruit(s)
        then true
        else contains_fruit(t)
```

```
contains_fruit :
  tree → bool
```

Write a shorter one.

1 We could have written this **if**-expression as `contains_fruit(s) orelse contains_fruit(t)`.

22 We can use *split_only*, which already checks whether a *tree* contains a Flat.

```
fun contains_fruit(x)
    = if¹ split_only(x)
        then false
        else true
```

1 We could have written this **if**-expression as `not(split_only(x))`.

What is the height of

```
Split(
 Split(
  Bud,
  Flat(Lemon,
   Bud)),
 Flat(Fig,
  Split(
   Bud,
   Bud)))?
```

23 3.

What is the height of

```
Split(
 Bud,
 Flat(Lemon,
  Bud))?
```

24 2.

What is the height of

```
Flat(Lemon,
 Bud)?
```

25 1.

What is the height of

```
Bud?
```

26 0.

So what is the height of a *tree*?

27 The height of a tree is the distance from the root to the highest bud in the tree.

Does *height* consume a *tree*?

28 Yes, and it produces an *int*.

What is the value of

```
height(
 Flat(Fig,
  Flat(Lemon,
   Flat(Apple,
    Bud))))?
```

29 3, isn't it?

---

30 What is the value of

```
height(
  Split(
    Split(
      Bud,
      Bud),
    Flat(Fig,
      Flat(Lemon,
        Flat(Apple,
          Bud)))))?
```

4.

---

31 Why is the height 4?

Because the value of

```
height(
  Split(
    Bud,
    Bud))
```

is 1, the value of

```
height(
  Flat(Fig,
    Flat(Lemon,
      Flat(Apple,
        Bud))))
```

is 3, and the larger of the two numbers is 3.

---

32 And how do we get from 3 to 4?

We need to add 1 to the larger of the numbers so that we don't forget the Split at the root of the tree.

---

33 Define the function *larger_of*.

What does it consume?

---

34 It consumes a pair of *int*s and produces an *int*.

```
larger_of :
  (int * int) → int
```

Well, then it must be this.

```
fun larger_of(n,m)
  = if less_than[1](n,m)
    then m
    else n
```

[1] You must define less_than as
`fun less_than(n:int,m:int) = (n < m).`

35 Here is *height*.

```
fun height(Bud)
    = 0
  | height(Flat(f,t))
    = 1 + height(t)
  | height(Split(s,t))
    = 1 + larger_of(height(s),height(t))
```

And here is its type.

```
height :
  tree → int
```

•

36 What is the value of
height(Split(Bud,Bud))?

1, of course.

37 And why is it 1?

Because *height*(Bud) is 0 and the larger of 0 and 0 is 0. And one more than 0 is 1.

38 What is the value of

```
subst_in_tree(Apple,Fig,
  Split(
    Split(
      Flat(Fig,
        Bud),
      Flat(Fig,
        Bud)),
    Flat(Fig,
      Flat(Lemon,
        Flat(Apple,
          Bud)))))?
```

That's also easy. We replace all Figs by Apples:

```
Split(
  Split(
    Flat(Apple,
      Bud),
    Flat(Apple,
      Bud)),
  Flat(Apple,
    Flat(Lemon,
      Flat(Apple,
        Bud)))).
```

Do we need to define *eq_fruit* before we define *subst_in_tree*? Here is its type.

```
eq_fruit :
  (fruit * fruit) → bool
```

39 How could you know, but we do need it!

```
fun eq_fruit(Peach,Peach)
      = true
  | eq_fruit(Apple,Apple)
      = true
  | eq_fruit(Pear,Pear)
      = true
  | eq_fruit(Lemon,Lemon)
      = true
  | eq_fruit(Fig,Fig)
      = true
  | eq_fruit(a_fruit,another_fruit)
      = false
```

How many lines would *eq_fruit* be if we had twenty-five different fruits?

40 When you have counted them all, you can have some apple juice.

Define the function *subst_in_tree*.

41 It's like *subst_fish* and *subst_int* from the end of chapter 5.

```
fun subst_in_tree(n,a,Bud)
      = Bud
  | subst_in_tree(n,a,Flat(f,t))
      = if eq_fruit(f,a)
          then Flat(n,subst_in_tree(n,a,t))
          else Flat(f,subst_in_tree(n,a,t))
  | subst_in_tree(n,a,Split(s,t))
      = Split(
          subst_in_tree(n,a,s),
          subst_in_tree(n,a,t))
```

```
subst_in_tree :
  (fruit * fruit * tree) → tree
```

42 How many times does Fig occur in

```
Split(
  Split(
    Flat(Fig,
      Bud),
    Flat(Fig,
      Bud)),
  Flat(Fig,
    Flat(Lemon,
      Flat(Apple,
        Bud))))?
```

3.

43 Write the function *occurs*.

This is so easy; just follow the patterns.

```
fun occurs(a,Bud)
    = 0
  | occurs(a,Flat(f,t))
    = if eq_fruit(f,a)
        then 1 + occurs(a,t)
        else occurs(a,t)
  | occurs(a,Split(s,t))
    = occurs(a,s) + occurs(a,t)
```

```
occurs :
  (fruit * tree) → int
```

44 Do you like your fruit with yogurt?

We prefer coconut sorbet.

45 Is it true that
An_atom(5)
is an *sexp*?

Yes,
because An_atom is one of the two constructors of *int sexp*.

46 Is it true that
An_atom(Fig)
is an *sexp*?

Yes,
because An_atom is one of the two constructors of *fruit sexp*.

Is it true that

A_slist(Empty)

is an *sexp*?

47 Yes,
because A_slist is the other constructor of *int sexp*.

Is it also true that

A_slist(Empty)

is an *sexp*?

48 Yes,
because A_slist is the other constructor of *fruit sexp*.

Is it true that

```
Scons(An_atom(5),
  Scons(An_atom(13),
    Scons(An_atom(1),
      Empty)))
```

is an *int slist*?

49 Yes,
because here Scons constructs *int slists* from *int sexps* and *int slists*.

Is it also true that

```
Scons(An_atom(Fig),
  Empty)
```

is a *fruit slist*?

50 Yes,
because Scons also constructs *fruit slist* from *fruit sexps* and *fruit slists*.

Okay, so here are two new shapes.

```
datatype
  α slist =
    Empty
  | Scons of ((α sexp) * (α slist))
and
  α sexp =
    An_atom of α
  | A_slist of (α slist)
```

What are the two shapes?

51 *α slist* and *α sexp*.

Why are the two definitions separated by **and**?

52 The first definition, *α slist*, refers to the second, *α sexp*; and the second refers to the first.

---

53 Do such mutually self-referential **datatypes** lead to mutually self-referential functions?

Always.

---

54 How many times does Fig occur in

```
Scons(An_atom(Fig),
  Scons(An_atom(Fig),
    Scons(An_atom(Lemon),
      Empty)))?
```

Twice.

---

55 What is the value of

```
occurs_in_slist(Fig,
  Scons(A_slist(
          Scons(An_atom(Fig),
            Scons(An_atom(Peach),
              Empty))),
    Scons(An_atom(Fig),
      Scons(An_atom(Lemon),
        Empty))))?
```

2, again.

---

56 And what does

```
occurs_in_sexp(Fig,
  A_slist(
    Scons(An_atom(Fig),
      Scons(An_atom(Peach),
        Empty))))
```

evaluate to?

1.

Here are the skeletons of *occurs_in_slist* and *occurs_in_sexp*.

```
fun
    occurs_in_slist(a,Empty)
    = ________
  | occurs_in_slist(a,Scons(s,y))
    = ________
and
    occurs_in_sexp(a,An_atom(b))
    = if eq_fruit(b,a)
        then 1
        else 0
  | occurs_in_sexp(a,A_slist(y))
    = ________
```

```
occurs_in_slist :
  (fruit * fruit slist) → int
```

Fill in the blanks. Also provide the type for *occurs_in_sexp*.

57 The blanks are easy now, because they just stand for the obvious answers.

```
fun
    occurs_in_slist(a,Empty)
    = 0
  | occurs_in_slist(a,Scons(s,y))
    = occurs_in_sexp(a,s) +
        occurs_in_slist(a,y)
and
    occurs_in_sexp(a,An_atom(b))
    = if eq_fruit(b,a)
        then 1
        else 0
  | occurs_in_sexp(a,A_slist(y))
    = occurs_in_slist(a,y)
```

```
occurs_in_sexp :
  (fruit * fruit sexp) → int
```

Define *subst_in_slist* and *subst_in_sexp*. Here are their types.

```
subst_in_slist :
  (fruit * fruit * fruit slist) → fruit slist
```

```
subst_in_sexp :
  (fruit * fruit * fruit sexp) → fruit sexp
```

58 That is no problem either.

```
fun
    subst_in_slist(n,a,Empty)
    = Empty
  | subst_in_slist(n,a,Scons(s,y))
    = Scons(
        subst_in_sexp(n,a,s),
        subst_in_slist(n,a,y))
and
    subst_in_sexp(n,a,An_atom(b))
    = if eq_fruit(b,a)
        then An_atom(n)
        else An_atom(b)
  | subst_in_sexp(n,a,A_slist(y))
    = A_slist(subst_in_slist(n,a,y))
```

Let's remove atoms. Here are the skeletons for *rem_from_slist* and *rem_from_sexp*.

```
fun
    rem_from_slist(a,Empty)
    = __________
  | rem_from_slist(a,Scons(s,y))
    = __________
and
    rem_from_sexp(a,An_atom(b))
    = __________
  | rem_from_sexp(a,A_slist(y))
    = __________
```

rem_from_slist :
(*fruit* ∗ *fruit slist*) → *fruit slist* •

rem_from_sexp :
(*fruit* ∗ *fruit sexp*) → *fruit sexp* •

59 Here are the obvious pieces.

```
fun
    rem_from_slist(a,Empty)
    = Empty
  | rem_from_slist(a,Scons(s,y))
    = __________
and
    rem_from_sexp(a,An_atom(b))
    = __________
  | rem_from_sexp(a,A_slist(y))
    = A_slist(rem_from_slist(a,y))
```

What is the value of
rem_from_sexp(Fig,
An_atom(Fig))?

60 It should be a *fruit sexp*, but there is no possible answer. No *sexp* is like An_atom(Fig) without Fig.

And what is the value of
rem_from_slist(Fig,
Scons(An_atom(Fig),
Empty))?

61 This is a related problem. The answer must be Empty, because that is the slist that is similar to
Scons(An_atom(Fig),
Empty)
without Fig.

When does *rem_from_slist* produce a slist that is shorter than the one it consumes?

62 When the first element in the slist is equal to the element to be removed.

Does that mean we should check in *rem_from_slist* whether the *sexp* inside of Scons is an atom?

63 Yes, we should check that and whether the atom is the one that is to be removed.

Here are the refined skeletons.

```
fun
    rem_from_slist(a,Empty)
    = Empty
  | rem_from_slist(a,Scons(s,y))
    = if eq_fruit_in_atom(a,s)
      then rem_from_slist(a,y)
      else Scons(
             rem_from_sexp(a,s),
             rem_from_slist(a,y))
and
    rem_from_sexp(a,An_atom(b))
    = __________
  | rem_from_sexp(a,A_slist(y))
    = A_slist(rem_from_slist(a,y))
```

Is *rem_from_sexp* ever applied to a fruit and an atom constructed from the same fruit?

64 We cannot know because we have never seen *eq_fruit_in_atom* before.

Voilà.

```
fun eq_fruit_in_atom(a,An_atom(s))
    = eq_fruit(a,s)
  | eq_fruit_in_atom(a_fruit,A_slist(y))
    = false
```

What is the type of *eq_fruit_in_atom*?

65 That's not difficult.

```
eq_fruit_in_atom :
  (fruit * fruit sexp) → bool
```

And what does it do?

66 It consumes a *fruit* and a *fruit sexp* and determines whether the latter is an atom constructed from the given *fruit*.

Is *rem_from_sexp* ever applied to a fruit and an atom constructed from the same fruit?

67 Not in *rem_from_slist*, because *rem_from_sexp* is only applied when *eq_fruit_in_atom*(*a*,*s*) is false.

68 What is the answer to the first pattern in *rem_from_sexp*?

Since it is never applied to two identical atoms, the answer is always An_atom(b). Hence, these are the complete mutually self-referential definitions.

```
fun
    rem_from_slist(a,Empty)
    = Empty
  | rem_from_slist(a,Scons(s,y))
    = if eq_fruit_in_atom(a,s)
      then rem_from_slist(a,y)
      else Scons(
             rem_from_sexp(a,s),
             rem_from_slist(a,y))
and
    rem_from_sexp(a,An_atom(b))
    = An_atom(b)
  | rem_from_sexp(a,A_slist(y))
    = A_slist(rem_from_slist(a,y))
```

69 Here are two skeletons that are similar to the first two.

```
fun
    rem_from_slist(a,Empty)
    = Empty
  | rem_from_slist(a,Scons(An_atom(b),y))
    = __________
and
    rem_from_sexp(a,An_atom(b))
    = __________
  | rem_from_sexp(a,A_slist(y))
    = A_slist(rem_from_slist(a,y))
```

What changed?

The only change is in the second pattern of *rem_from_slist*. The new pattern says that the first item of the slist must be an atom.

70 What is the answer that corresponds to that pattern?

The answer depends on a and b. If they are the same, it is

rem_from_slist(a,y)

otherwise, it is

Scons(An_atom(b),*rem_from_slist*(a,y)).

Can *rem_from_slist* match all possible α *slists*?

71 No, not if the first element is an α *sexp* that was constructed by A_slist.

Let's add another pattern to the skeletons.

72 Something like this.

```
fun
    rem_from_slist(a,Empty)
    = Empty
  | rem_from_slist(a,Scons(An_atom(b),y))
    = if eq_fruit(a,b)
        then rem_from_slist(a,y)
        else Scons(
               An_atom(b),
               rem_from_slist(a,y))
  | rem_from_slist(a,Scons(A_slist(x),y))
    = __________
and
    rem_from_sexp(a,An_atom(b))
    = __________
  | rem_from_sexp(a,A_slist(y))
    = A_slist(rem_from_slist(a,y))
```

What is the answer for the last pattern in *rem_from_slist*?

73 We need to remove all a's from the slist x and from the slist y.

Does that mean we can use

rem_from_slist(a,x)

and

rem_from_slist(a,y)?

74 Yes.

And what do we do with the results?

75 We Scons them back together again.

Refine the skeletons.

76 Once we fill in the blank in *rem_from_slist*, we no longer need *rem_from_sexp*. Here is the complete definition.

```
fun rem_from_slist(a,Empty)
    = Empty
  | rem_from_slist(a,Scons(An_atom(b),y))
    = if eq_fruit(a,b)
        then rem_from_slist(a,y)
        else Scons(
               An_atom(b),
               rem_from_slist(a,y))
  | rem_from_slist(a,Scons(A_slist(x),y))
    = Scons(
        A_slist(rem_from_slist(a,x)),
        rem_from_slist(a,y))
```

Describe in your own words what we just discovered.

77 Here are our words:
"After we have designed a program that naturally follows the **datatype** definitions, we can considerably improve it by focusing on its weaknesses and carefully rearranging its pieces."

The Sixth Moral

As datatype definitions get more complicated, so do the functions over them.

7. Functions Are People, Too

What is the type of this function?

```
fun identity(x)
  = x
```

1 Whatever it consumes is what it produces.

```
identity :
  α → α
```

What does $\alpha \to \alpha$ mean?

2 It means that *identity* is a function that consumes and produces values of the same type, no matter what the type is.

What does "no matter what the type is" mean?

3 Here are our words:
"Pick an arbitrary type. Then, *identity* consumes and produces values of the chosen type."

And what does the word "arbitrary" mean?

4 Our words again.
"It means that there is no relationship between the type that you choose and the type that we choose."

What is the type of *true_maker*?

```
fun true_maker(x)
  = true
```

5 It always produces true.

```
true_maker :
  α → bool
```

Was that easy?

6 Of course, *true_maker* consumes values of any type and always produces a *bool*.

Make up a value of the type *bool_or_int*.

```
datatype bool_or_int =
  Hot of bool
| Cold of int
```

7 Here is one: Hot(true).

What is the type of Hot(true)? | 8 *bool_or_int*.

And how about another value of this type? | 9 Cold(10).

What is the type of Cold(5)? | 10 *bool_or_int*.

What is the type of *hot_maker*?

```
fun hot_maker(x)
    = Hot
```

11 It must also start with α, because it can consume anything.

And what does it produce? | 12 It produces Hot.

What is the type of Hot(true)? | 13 *bool_or_int*, as we mentioned earlier.

What is the type of true? | 14 *bool*.

So Hot is of type ... | 15 ... *bool* $\rightarrow$ *bool_or_int*.

Does that mean Hot is a function? | 16 Yes, absolutely.

Did we just agree that constructors are functions?

17 Those constructors that are followed by **of** in the **datatype** definition are indeed functions.

Then what is the type of *hot_maker*?

18 It must be this.

```
hot_maker :
  α → (bool → bool_or_int)
```

•

---

19 Does that mean *hot_maker* is a function?

Yes, we defined it that way.

20 Here is *help*, a new function definition.

```
fun help(f)
    = Hot(
        true_maker(
          if true_maker(________)
            then f
            else true_maker))
```

```
help :
  (α → bool) → bool_or_int
```

Does it matter whether the blank is replaced by true or 5?

No,
because *true_maker* consumes all types of values, *e.g.*, true, 6, Hot, and so on.

```
fun help(f)
    = Hot(
        true_maker(
          if true_maker(5)
            then f
            else true_maker))
```

21 What is the difference between

$\alpha \rightarrow (bool \rightarrow bool\_or\_int)$

and

$(\alpha \rightarrow bool) \rightarrow bool\_or\_int$?

The difference is the placement of the matching parentheses. In the first type, the parentheses enclose the last two types, *bool* and *bool_or_int*, and in the second type the parentheses enclose the first two types, α and *bool*.

22 Are they really different?

Yes, one consumes a function and the other produces one.

23 Does that mean functions can consume functions?

Yes, and, as we have already seen, they can produce them, too.

24 Does that mean functions are values?

Yes, functions are values, too.

25 How do we determine the type of the values that *help* produces?

That's easy. We know that Hot always returns a *bool_or_int*, which means that *help* must be of type

____ → *bool_or_int*.

How do we determine the type of the values that *help* consumes?	26	That's tricky.
What is the type of the values that Hot consumes?	27	*bool*.
Does *true_maker* produce a *bool*?	28	Yes, it does. We said so earlier.
Is it important that Hot consumes *bool*s and that *true_maker* produces them?	29	Yes, because whatever *true_maker* produces is consumed by Hot in the definition of *help*.
What is the type of the values that *true_maker* consumes?	30	It consumes values of any type and therefore it doesn't matter how we fill in the blank.
What is the type of **if** *true_maker*(_________) **then** *f* **else** *true_maker*?	31	It doesn't matter, because the result of this expression is consumed by *true_maker* and *true_maker* consumes values of any type.
Does it matter that **if** *true_maker*(_________) **then** *f* **else** *true_maker* has a type?	32	Although it doesn't matter which type it has, it matters a lot that it has a type. If the expression didn't have a type, it would be nonsense.
How do we determine the type of **if** exp_1 **then** exp_2 **else** exp_3?	33	It is the type of exp_2 or the type of exp_3, because their types must be the same.
What is the type of *true_maker*?	34	$\alpha \rightarrow bool$.

What is the type of f?

35 It doesn't have one yet. Therefore we can say that f's type is $\alpha \rightarrow bool$, because f and *true_maker* must have the same type.

Do we know enough now to determine the type of *help*?

36 Yes, we do. The type of f is the type of what is consumed, and the type of what is produced by Hot is *bool_or_int*. Therefore the type of *help* is

$(\alpha \rightarrow bool) \rightarrow bool\_or\_int$.

Should we go through this again?

37 Perhaps someone should.

Look at this **datatype** definition.

```
datatype chain =
  Link of (int * (int → chain))
```

What is unusual about it?

38 It is the first **datatype** definition that has only one alternative. It is also the first **datatype** definition to use →.

Is the definition self-referential?

39 Yes, because *chain* appears in its own definition.

Have we seen self-referential **datatypes** before?

40 Sure, many of them were.

How do they differ from this one?

41 This **datatype** definition includes only self-referential alternatives, whereas the others always contain at least one alternative that is not.

Make up a value of type *chain*.

42 That seems impossible. The basic alternatives—those without a self-reference—in the previous **datatype** definitions always provide us with a starting point for the creation of values. The **datatype** definition of *chain* has no starting point.

What does that mean?

43 Every value of type *chain* is a pair. The first component of the pair must be an *int*. That part is easy. But, the second component must be a function.

Haven't we just seen that functions are values?

44 Yes, but the kind of function we need now is strange.

What is strange about it?

45 It consumes an *int*, which is also easy, but it produces a *chain*, which brings us back to the original problem.

Does that mean the function's type is $int \to chain$?

46 That is what the **datatype** requires.

Here is a start at such a function.

```
fun ints(n)
  = Link(n + 1, ________)
```

What is the type of *ints*?

47 It clearly consumes an *int* and the answer it constructs is a *chain*.

```
ints :
  int → chain
```

How must we fill in the blank?

48 As we said before, the blank must be filled in with a function of type $int \to chain$.

Don't we have such a function?

49 Only one: *ints*.

Fill in the blank now.

50 Now it is easy.

```
fun ints(n)
  = Link(n + 1,ints)
```

What is the value of *ints*(0)?

51 Link(1,*ints*).

Why?

52 Because n stands for 0 and the answer is Link(0 + 1,*ints*).

What is the value of *ints*(5)?

53 Link(6,*ints*).

What is the value of *ints*(13)?

54 Link(14,*ints*).

What is the value of *ints*(50005)?

55 Link(50006,*ints*).

How many times can we do this?

56 Lots. As many as there are *int*s.

Did you notice the roman "s" at the end of *int*?

57 If not, start over.

What is the type of this function?

```
fun skips(n)
    = Link(n + 2,skips)
```

58 This function also consumes *int*s and produces *chain*s.

```
skips :
  int → chain
```

What is the value of *skips*(8)?

59 Link(10,*skips*).

60 What is the value of
skips(17)?

Link(19,*skips*).

---

61 What are the types of these functions?

```
fun divides_evenly(n,c)
    = eq_int((n mod c),0)
```

```
fun is_mod_5_or_7(n)
    = if divides_evenly(n,5)
        then true
        else divides_evenly(n,7)
```

The types are easy, if *mod* consumes a pair of *ints*.

```
divides_evenly :
  (int * int) → bool
```

```
is_mod_5_or_7 :
  int → bool
```

---

62 Here is another function that produces a *chain*.

```
fun some_ints(n)
    = if is_mod_5_or_7(n + 1)
        then Link(n + 1,some_ints)
        else some_ints(n + 1)
```

```
some_ints :
  int → chain
```

Okay.

---

63 What are the values of
some_ints(1),
some_ints(17),
and
some_ints(116)?

No problem:
Link(5,*some_ints*),
Link(20,*some_ints*),
and
Link(119,*some_ints*).

---

64 And why are these the right answers?

Because 5, 20, and 119 are evenly divisible by 5 or 7.

Is that it?	65 Tea break, anyone?
What is the first *int* in the chain *ints*(0)?	66 It's obviously 1.
How about the second?	67 That's not obvious. Every Link contains an *int* and a function. There isn't really a second *int*.
Yet, we know that it is 2, don't we?	68 Yes, we know: "Because we may think of *ints* as a very long sequence of *ints*. We go from one element in this sequence to the next by applying the second component of *ints*(n) to the first."
And what do we get here?	69 Link(2,*ints*).
Is it true then that the third *int* is 3?	70 Yes, it is 3 in the very same sense.
What is the first *some_int* in the chain *some_ints*(0)?	71 5.
How about the second?	72 That's not obvious. Every Link contains a number and a function. There isn't really a second *some_int*.
Yet, we know that it is 7, don't we?	73 Yes, if we apply the second component of *some_ints*(0) to the first, we get Link(7,*some_ints*).

What is *some_ints*(0)?

74 It is a *chain* of all those numbers (larger than 1) that are evenly divisible by 5 or 7.

How many patterns do we need for a function that consumes *chains*?

75 One,
because there is only one alternative in the **datatype** definition of *chain*.

Fill in the blanks in this skeleton.

```
fun chain_item(n,Link(i,f))
  = if eq_int(n,1)
      then ________
      else chain_item(n - 1,________)
```

```
chain_item :
  (int * chain) → int                    •
```

76 The first blank is easy. The result must be an *int*, so it can only be i or n. Since we know that n is 1, we pick i.

Why is i a good answer and not just an answer of the right type?

77 We are looking for the nth *int* in the *chain*. Since i is the first (*i.e.*, 1st) element of the *chain*, the result is i when n is 1.

Could the answer have been 17?

78 The type is right, but who would want to define a function that always returns 17?

What is the type of the second blank?

79 It must be *chain*, because *chain_item* consumes a pair consisting of an *int* and a *chain*.

What are our possibilities?

80 The type of Link(i,f) is *chain*. But, since f is of type

int → *chain*,

$f(i)$ is also of type *chain*.

81 Is Link(i,f) an interesting possibility?

No,
because *chain_item* would always receive a pair with the same second component, so the answer would always be the first *int* in the *chain*.

---

82 So the blank must be filled with $f(i)$, right?

Yes, because a *chain* consists of an *int* and a function that consumes that value to produce the next chain.

---

83 Complete the definition of *chain_item*.

```
fun chain_item(n,Link(i,f))
    = if eq_int(n,1)
        then i
        else chain_item(n − 1,________)
```

Here it is.

```
fun chain_item(n,Link(i,f))
    = if eq_int(n,1)
        then i
        else chain_item(n − 1,f(i))
```

---

84 How do we find the 1st, 6th, and 37th elements of *some_ints*(0)?

We determine the values of

chain_item(1,*some_ints*(0)),

chain_item(6,*some_ints*(0)),

and

chain_item(37,*some_ints*(0)).

---

85 And what are the values?

They are 5, 20, and 119, respectively.

---

86 Easy?

If you didn't take a tea break before, how about some coffee now?

---

87 What is the next number in this sequence?
2, 3, 5, 7, 11, 13, 17, 19, 23, 29, 31, ...

37.

---

88 Why?

It is the next prime number.

What is a prime number?

89 A number is prime if it is (strictly) greater than 1 and can be divided evenly only by itself and 1.

What is the value of *is_prime*(3)?

90 true, of course.

What is the value of *is_prime*(81)?

91 false, because it can be divided evenly by 3.

Let's get started on *is_prime*.

```
fun
    is_prime(n)
    = has_no_divisors(n,n - 1)
and
    has_no_divisors(n,c)
    = ...
```

⊗

What is the type of *is_prime*?

92 It consumes *ints* and produces *bools*.

Define *has_no_divisors*, which goes through all the numbers from *c*, the second value it consumes, down to 2 and tests whether *n*, the first value consumed, is evenly divisible by any of them. If so, it produces false; otherwise, it produces true.

93 In that case, *c* must vary.

```
fun
    is_prime(n)
    = has_no_divisors(n,n - 1)
and
    has_no_divisors(n,c)
    = if eq_int(c,1)
        then true
        else
          if divides_evenly(n,c)
            then false
            else has_no_divisors(n,c - 1)
```

Why do we use **and** to combine two definitions?[1]

[1] You could also have written

```
local
 fun has_no_divisors(n,c)
    = if eq_int(c,1)
       then true
       else
        if divides_evenly(n,c)
         then false
         else has_no_divisors(n,c - 1)
in
 fun is_prime(n)
    = has_no_divisors(n,n - 1)
end
```

...

94 Because the first definition is more important than the second one and yet it refers to the second one.[1]

[1] ...or

```
fun is_prime(n)
   = let
      fun has_no_divisors(n,c)
         = if eq_int(c,1)
            then true
            else
             if divides_evenly(n,c)
              then false
              else has_no_divisors(n,c - 1)
     in
      has_no_divisors(n,n - 1)
     end
```

Do we now know what the types of *is_prime* and *has_no_divisors* are?

95 Now it is easy because we know that *has_no_divisors* produces a *bool*.

is_prime **:**
  int → *bool* •

has_no_divisors **:**
  (*int* ∗ *int*) → *bool* •

Here is another long chain link.

fun *primes*(*n*)
  = **if** *is_prime*(*n* + 1)
    then Link(*n* + 1,*primes*)
    else *primes*(*n* + 1)

primes **:**
  int → *chain* •

What is the value of
  chain_item(12,*primes*(1))?

96 37.

Do you like rabbits?

97 Perhaps not to eat but to pet.

Here is how to make more rabbits.[1]

```
fun fibs(n)(m)
    = Link(n + m,fibs(m))
```

What does *fibs* consume?

[1] In the *Liber abaci*, Leonardo of Pisa (1175–1250), also known as Fibonacci, describes the following problem. A pair of rabbits is placed in a pen to find out how many offspring will be produced by this pair in one year if each pair of rabbits gives birth to a new pair of rabbits each month starting with the second month of its life. The solution is known as the Fibonacci Sequence of numbers.

98 It seems to consume two things, called n and m. Since we add them together, they must be *ints*.

What does *fibs* produce?

99 That's easier. It produces a chain.

So why isn't this the type of *fibs*?

```
fibs:
  (int * int) → chain
```
⊗

100 Because there is no comma between n and m; instead there is)(.

What must be the type of *fibs*(n)?

101 We know that Link consumes an *int* and a function from *int* to *chain*. So, *fibs*(n) must be a function from *int* to *chain*.

So what is the type of *fibs*?

102 It really consumes just one *int*.

And then?

103 It produces a function from *int* to *chain*.

So what is the type of *fibs*?

104 Now it is obvious.

```
fibs :
  int → (int → chain)
```
•

Yes, and we just found out about another notation for building functions that return functions.

105 Yes, we did.

What is the value of
  Link(0,*fibs*(1))?

106 If you know this, take a short nap.

To determine its value, we only need to know the value of *fibs*(1).

107 Yes, but what is it?

What type of thing is *fibs*(1)?

108 It is a function of type $int \rightarrow chain$.

Here is such a function.

```
fun fibs_1(m)
    = Link(1 + m,fibs(m))
```

Where does it come from?

109 It is like *fibs*, without (n).

What showed up in place of n?

110 Every place where n appeared in the definition, except behind *fibs*, there is a 1 now.

We think of *fibs_1* as the value of *fibs*(1).

111 That is simple enough.

What is the value of
  fibs(1)($\underline{1}$)?

112 The same as the value of
  fibs_1($\underline{1}$).

Do you see the underscores under the 1's?

113 Yes, and the 1 without an underscore has been consumed in the process.

114 What is the value of *fibs_1*(1)?

Link(2,*fibs_1*), a chain.

---

115 What is the value of *fibs_1*(2)?

The same as the value of Link(3,*fibs*(2)).

---

116 What is the value of *fibs*(2)?

It is a function from *int* to *chain*.

---

117 Define *fibs_2*.

This is easy as pie.

```
fun fibs_2(m)
    = Link(2 + m,fibs(m))
```

---

118 Don't forget the ice cream!

Okay.

The Seventh Moral

Some functions consume values of arrow type; some produce values of arrow type.

8.
Bows and Arrows

Do you know *fish lists* and *int lists*?

1 The datatype definition of *list* is an old family friend of ours.

```
datatype α list =
   Empty
 | Cons of α * α list
```

Can you compare apples to oranges?

2 No, how could we do that?

First, we put them together in a new datatype.

```
datatype orapl¹ =
   Orange
 | Apple
```

[1] A better name for this is orange_or_apple.

3 Then comparing them is easy.

```
fun eq_orapl(Orange,Orange)
    = true
  | eq_orapl(Apple,Apple)
    = true
  | eq_orapl(one,another)
    = false
```

```
eq_orapl :
  (orapl * orapl) → bool
```

Here is *subst_int*.

```
fun subst_int(n,a,Empty)
    = Empty
  | subst_int(n,a,Cons(e,t))
    = if eq_int(a,e)
        then Cons(n,subst_int(n,a,t))
        else Cons(e,subst_int(n,a,t))
```

```
subst_int :
  (int * int * int list) → int list
```

Define *subst_orapl*.

4 It basically looks like *subst_int* and has a similar type.

```
fun subst_orapl(n,a,Empty)
    = Empty
  | subst_orapl(n,a,Cons(e,t))
    = if eq_orapl(a,e)
        then Cons(n,subst_orapl(n,a,t))
        else Cons(e,subst_orapl(n,a,t))
```

```
subst_orapl :
  (orapl * orapl * orapl list) → orapl list
```

Would *subst_bool* be more difficult to define?

5 No, we would have to substitute *bool* for *int* everywhere in *subst_int*.

Would *subst_num* be more difficult to define?

6 No, we would have to substitute *num* for *int* everywhere in *subst_int*.

Would *subst_fish* be more difficult to define?

7 No, we would have to substitute *fish* for *int* everywhere in *subst_int*.

Are you tired of all this duplication yet?

8 Yes, is this going somewhere?

Okay, so let's not duplicate this work over and over again.

```
fun subst(rel¹,n,a,Empty)
    = Empty
  | subst(rel,n,a,Cons(e,t))
    = if rel(a,e)
        then Cons(n,subst(rel,n,a,t))
        else Cons(e,subst(rel,n,a,t))
```

What is the type of *subst*?

[1] A better name for `rel` is `relation`.

9 It is a function that consumes a value with four components, and that's what we can see immediately:

$$(\_\_\_\_ * \_\_\_\_ * \_\_\_\_ * \_\_\_\_) \rightarrow \_\_\_\_.$$

What do we know about the last component that *subst* consumes?

10 It must be a list, but since we don't know what kind of elements the list contains, we use α *list*:

$$(\_\_\_\_ * \_\_\_\_ * \_\_\_\_ * \alpha\ list) \rightarrow \_\_\_\_.$$

How is the type of the result related to that of the fourth component?

11 If *rel* always produced false, then the answer would have to be identical to the fourth component consumed. So, the type on the right of $\rightarrow$ must be α *list*:

$$(\_\_\_\_ * \_\_\_\_ * \_\_\_\_ * \alpha\ list) \rightarrow \alpha\ list.$$

What does α mean here?

12 If *subst* consumes an *int list*, it produces an *int list*; if it consumes a *num list*, it produces a *num list*; and if it consumes a (*num list*) *list*, it produces a (*num list*) *list*; and if it consumes an *orapl list*, it produces an *orapl list*.

Does that imply anything else?

13 Yes, since exp_2 and exp_3 in

if exp_1
  then exp_2
  else exp_3

are of the same type, this also means that n and e are of the same type. Since e is an element of the consumed list and is therefore of type α, so is n:

$(\_\_\_\_ * \alpha * \_\_\_\_ * \alpha\ list) \rightarrow \alpha\ list.$

Does that mean the type of a is α?

14 Who knows? We don't know what *rel* consumes.

Does that mean we don't know what kind of value it is?

15 Yes, and so we could agree that its type is β:

$(\_\_\_\_ * \alpha * \beta * \alpha\ list) \rightarrow \alpha\ list.$

When is α different from β?

16 On occasion, β will stand for the same type as α, and sometimes it will be a different type.

What is the type of *rel*?

17 It is a function that obviously produces *bool* and consumes a β and an α. And we don't know anything more about its type.

> *subst* **:**
> $(((\beta * \alpha) \rightarrow bool) * \alpha * \beta * \alpha\ list)$
> $\rightarrow \alpha\ list$
> •

Describe in your words what that type says about *subst*.

18 You knew that we would use *our* words: "The type says that *subst* consumes a value with four components: a function, an arbitrary value of type α, another arbitrary value of type β, and a list. But, all elements in the list must have the type α, and the function must consume pairs of type $\beta * \alpha$."

Anything else?

19 Of course, the result of *subst* is a list whose elements are of the same type as the first arbitrary value.

Suppose we want to substitute one *int* in a list of *ints* by some other *int*.

20 Then, we need to give *subst* a function that consumes two *ints* as its first argument.

Do we know of such a function?

21 Yes, we do: *eq_int*.

So how do we use *subst* to substitute all occurrences of 15 in

```
Cons(15,
  Cons(6,
    Cons(15,
      Cons(17,
        Cons(15,
          Cons(8,
            Empty))))))
```

by 11?

22 We use *eq_int* as *rel* and otherwise act as if we were using *subst_int*:

```
subst(eq_int,11,15,
  Cons(15,
    Cons(6,
      Cons(15,
        Cons(17,
          Cons(15,
            Cons(8,
              Empty))))))).
```

And that produces?

23 A list with three 11's.

```
Cons(11,
  Cons(6,
    Cons(11,
      Cons(17,
        Cons(11,
          Cons(8,
            Empty)))))).
```

What is the value of
less_than(15,17)?

24 true.

Is *less_than* a function that consumes a two-component value with both components being *ints*?

25 Yes, that's right.

Can we use it with *subst*?

26 Yes, we can substitute all *ints* in an *int list* that are greater than or equal to some other *int*.

So how would we substitute all numbers not less than 15 in

```
Cons(15,
 Cons(6,
  Cons(15,
   Cons(17,
    Cons(15,
     Cons(8,
      Empty))))))
```

by 11?

27 We use *less_than* as *rel* and otherwise act as if we were using *subst_int*:

```
subst(less_than,11,15,
 Cons(15,
  Cons(6,
   Cons(15,
    Cons(17,
     Cons(15,
      Cons(8,
       Empty))))))).
```

And what does that produce?

28 A list with an 11:

```
Cons(15,
 Cons(6,
  Cons(15,
   Cons(11,
    Cons(15,
     Cons(8,
      Empty)))))).
```

What is the value of
in_range((11,16),15)?

29 true.

What does *in_range* do?

30 It determines whether or not some number is in some range of numbers.

So what is the value of
in_range((11,15),15)?

31 false.

Why is it false?

32 Because 15 is not less than 15. Is
in_range((15,22),15)
also false?

Yes, same deal.

33 Then the function is easy to define.

```
fun in_range((small,large),x)
   = if less_than(small,x)
       then less_than(x,large)
       else false
```

```
in_range :
 ((int * int) * int) → bool
```

•

Is *in_range* a function that consumes a value whose components are a pair of *int*s and an *int*?

34 That's what its type says.

Can we use it with *subst*?

35 We could as long as the third component consumed by *subst* is a pair of *int*s.

So how would we substitute all numbers between 11 and 16 in

```
Cons(15,
  Cons(6,
    Cons(15,
      Cons(17,
        Cons(15,
          Cons(8,
            Empty))))))
```

by 22?

36 We use *in_range* as *rel*:

```
subst(in_range,22,(11,16),
  Cons(15,
    Cons(6,
      Cons(15,
        Cons(17,
          Cons(15,
            Cons(8,
              Empty))))))).
```

And what does that produce?

37 A list with three 22's:

```
Cons(22,
  Cons(6,
    Cons(22,
      Cons(17,
        Cons(22,
          Cons(8,
            Empty)))))).
```

Does that mean α and β are different for this use of *subst*?

38 They sure are. Here α stands for *int* and β for (*int* $*$ *int*).

Have an orange.

39 No, an apple is better.

Can we do all these things with *subst_pred*?

```
fun subst_pred(pred,n,Empty)
    = Empty
  | subst_pred(pred,n,Cons(e,t))
    = if pred(e)
        then Cons(n,subst_pred(pred,n,t))
        else Cons(e,subst_pred(pred,n,t))
```

40 Shouldn't we determine *subst_pred*'s type first?[1]

[1] A better name for `subst_pred` is `substitute_using_a_predicate`.

Okay let's figure out its type.

41 This function consumes a value with only three components, so its type is shorter than that of *subst*:

$$(\_\_\_\_ * \_\_\_\_ * \_\_\_\_) \rightarrow \_\_\_\_.$$

Is the result still an α *list*?

42 Sure, and so is the last component of the value consumed:

$$(\_\_\_\_ * \_\_\_\_ * \alpha\ list) \rightarrow \alpha\ list.$$

Does that mean the second one is of type α, too?

43 Yes, and it follows from the same reasoning that we used to determine the type for *subst*:

$$(\_\_\_\_ * \alpha * \alpha\ list) \rightarrow \alpha\ list.$$

44 And what is *pred*?

It is a function that consumes one value, an element of the list, and produces a *bool*.

subst_pred :
$((\alpha \rightarrow bool) * \alpha * \alpha\ list) \rightarrow \alpha\ list$ •

45 Describe in your words what that type says about *subst_pred*.

Here are our words again:
"The type says that *subst_pred* consumes a value with three components: a function, an arbitrary value of type α, and a list. But, all elements in the list must have type α, and the function must consume values of that type."

46 Anything else?

Same as before. The result of *subst_pred* is a list whose elements are of the same type as the arbitrary value.

47 So how do we use *subst_pred* to substitute all occurrences of 15 in

```
Cons(15,
 Cons(6,
  Cons(15,
   Cons(17,
    Cons(15,
     Cons(8,
      Empty))))))
```

by 11?

We need a function that compares the value it consumes to 15.

48 Define this function.

Easy.

```
fun is_15(n)
    = eq_int(n,15)
```

is_15 :
$int \rightarrow bool$ •

So how do we use *subst_pred* to substitute all occurrences of 15 in

```
Cons(15,
 Cons(6,
  Cons(15,
   Cons(17,
    Cons(15,
     Cons(8,
      Empty))))))
```

by 11?

49 We use *is_15* as *pred* and otherwise act as if we were using *subst_int*:

```
subst_pred(is_15,11,
 Cons(15,
  Cons(6,
   Cons(15,
    Cons(17,
     Cons(15,
      Cons(8,
       Empty))))))).
```

And that produces?

50 Same as above:

```
Cons(11,
 Cons(6,
  Cons(11,
   Cons(17,
    Cons(11,
     Cons(8,
      Empty)))))).
```

What is the value of *less_than_15*(11)?

51 true.

Define *less_than_15*.

52 Easy, too.

```
fun less_than_15(x)
  = less_than(x,15)
```

```
less_than_15 :
 int → bool
```

Is *less_than_15* a function that consumes an *int*?

53 That's what its type says.

Can we use it with *subst_pred*?

54 Yes, we can to substitute all *int*s in an *int list* that are less than 15.

So how would we substitute all numbers less than 15 in

```
Cons(15,
  Cons(6,
    Cons(15,
      Cons(17,
        Cons(15,
          Cons(8,
            Empty))))))
```

by 11?

55 We use *less_than_15* as *pred* and otherwise act as if we were using *subst_int*:

```
subst_pred(less_than_15,11,
  Cons(15,
    Cons(6,
      Cons(15,
        Cons(17,
          Cons(15,
            Cons(8,
              Empty))))))).
```

And what does that produce?

56 A list with two 11's:

```
Cons(15,
  Cons(11,
    Cons(15,
      Cons(17,
        Cons(15,
          Cons(11,
            Empty)))))).
```

What is the value of
in_range_11_16(15)?

57 true.

What does *in_range_11_16* do?

58 It determines whether or not some number is in the range between 11 and 16.

Define *in_range_11_16*.

59 Whew, another easy one.

```
fun in_range_11_16(x)
  = if less_than(11,x)
    then less_than(x,16)
    else false
```

```
in_range_11_16 :
  int → bool
```

•

Does *in_range* consume an *int*?

60 That's what its type says.

Can we use it with *subst_pred*?

61 Well, we could as long as the third component consumed by *subst_pred* is an *int list*.

So how would we substitute all numbers between 11 and 16 in

```
Cons(15,
  Cons(6,
    Cons(15,
      Cons(17,
        Cons(15,
          Cons(8,
            Empty))))))
```

by 22?

62 We use *in_range_11_16* as *pred*:

```
subst_pred(in_range_11_16,22,
  Cons(15,
    Cons(6,
      Cons(15,
        Cons(17,
          Cons(15,
            Cons(8,
              Empty))))))).
```

And what does that produce?

63 A list with three 22's:

```
Cons(22,
  Cons(6
    Cons(22,
      Cons(17,
        Cons(22,
          Cons(8,
            Empty)))))).
```

We recommend dinner now. How about some Indian lamb?

64 Don't forget the curry.

Did you have your fill of curry? Then take a look at this variant of *in_range_11_16*.

```
fun in_range_c(small,large)(x)
  = if less_than(small,x)
      then less_than(x,large)
      else false
```

What is different about it besides its name?

65 It is like *in_range_11_16*, but it doesn't contain 11 and 16. Instead, it first consumes a pair of *int*s and then another *int*.[1]

[1] Such functions are said to be *curried*. A better name for this function would be `in_range_Curry` after Haskell B. Curry (1900–1982) and Moses Schönfinkel (1889-1942).

So what is the type of *in_range_c*?

66 We need to substitute just one $*$ with an $\rightarrow$ in the type of *in_range*.

> *in_range_c* **:**
> $(int * int) \rightarrow \underline{(}int \rightarrow bool\underline{)}$
> •

What is the purpose of the underlined parentheses?

67 They surround the type of what *in_range_c* produces.

Does that mean that *in_range_c* is a function that consumes one pair of *int*s?

68 Yes, and it produces a function.

What does the function that it produces consume?

69 That function consumes an *int*, just like *in_range_11_16*.

What is the value of

in_range_c(11,16)?

70 It is a function, and that function is just like *in_range_11_16*.

Can you define a function that is like

in_range_c(11,16)?

71 We copy *in_range_c* and substitute 11 for *small* and 16 for *large*.

```
fun in_range_c_11_16(x)
    = if less_than(11,x)
        then less_than(x,16)
        else false
```

So what is the difference between

in_range_11_16

and

in_range_c_11_16?

72 None.

Is there a difference between

in_range_11_16

and

in_range_c(11,16)?

73 No, there really isn't. Are they equal?

Yes, but no function can determine that they are equal.

74 What does that mean?

It means that no one can define the function *eq_int_funcs*, which consumes two functions from *int* to *int* and determines whether the two functions are equal.

75 That's interesting. Since functions from *int* to *int* are pretty simple, does that imply that there is no general function *eq_funcs*?

Yes, but let's move on. So how would we substitute all numbers between 11 and 16 in

```
Cons(15,
 Cons(6,
  Cons(15,
   Cons(17,
    Cons(15,
     Cons(8,
      Empty))))))
```

by 22?

76 We use *in_range_c*(11,16) as *pred*:

```
subst_pred(in_range_c(11,16),22,
 Cons(15,
  Cons(6,
   Cons(15,
    Cons(17,
     Cons(15,
      Cons(8,
       Empty))))))).
```

How would we substitute all numbers between 3 and 16 in

```
Cons(15,
 Cons(6,
  Cons(15,
   Cons(17,
    Cons(15,
     Cons(8,
      Empty))))))
```

by 22?

77 We use *in_range_c*(3,16) as *pred*:

```
subst_pred(in_range_c(3,16),22,
 Cons(15,
  Cons(6,
   Cons(15,
    Cons(17,
     Cons(15,
      Cons(8,
       Empty))))))).
```

Can we also substitute all numbers in the range between 11 and 27?

78 Of course, we could but we are hungry again. How about you?

Did you have your fill of curry now? If not, take a look at this new variant of *subst_pred*.

```
fun subst_c(pred)(n,Empty)
    = Empty
  | subst_c(pred)(n,Cons(e,t))
    = if pred(e)
        then Cons(n,subst_c(pred)(n,t))
        else Cons(e,subst_c(pred)(n,t))
```

What is different about it besides its name?

79 It is like *subst_pred* but it consumes values in two stages. First, it consumes *pred*, then *n* and a list.[1]

[1] To emphasize the two-stage aspect, we could write

```
fun subst_c(pred)
  = fn (n,Empty)
    => Empty
     | (n,Cons(e,t))
    => if pred(e)
         then Cons(n,subst_c(pred)(n,t))
         else Cons(e,subst_c(pred)(n,t))
```

So what is the type of *subst_c*?

80 We need to substitute just one $*$ with an $\rightarrow$ in the type of *subst_pred*.

subst_c **:**
$(\alpha \rightarrow bool) \rightarrow \underline{(}(\alpha * (\alpha\ list)) \rightarrow \alpha\ list\underline{)}$ •

What is the purpose of the underlined parentheses?

81 As before, they surround the type of what *subst_c* produces.

Does that mean that *subst_c* is a function that consumes one thing?

82 Yes, it consumes a function and produces one.

What does the function that it produces consume?

83 That function consumes a pair.

Can you define a function that is like

subst_c(*in_range_c*(11,16))?

84 We know that the value of

in_range_c(11,16)

is just like *in_range_11_16*.

Which means that we should have asked you to define a function that is like

subst_c(*in_range_11_16*)?

85 Yes.

Define *subst_c_in_range_11_16*.

86 What an obvious name. We copy *subst_c*, delete (*pred*) five times, and substitute *in_range_11_16* three times for the uses of *pred*.

```
fun subst_c_in_range_11_16(n,Empty)
    = Empty
  | subst_c_in_range_11_16(n,Cons(e,t))
    = if in_range_11_16(e)
        then
          Cons(n,
            subst_c_in_range_11_16(n,t))
        else
          Cons(e,
            subst_c_in_range_11_16(n,t))
```

We had tea much too.

87 How about you?

Simplify the following definition.

```
fun combine(Empty,Empty)
    = Empty
  | combine(Empty,Cons(b,l2))
    = Cons(b,l2)
  | combine(Cons(a,l1),Empty)
    = Cons(a,l1)
  | combine(Cons(a,l1),Cons(b,l2))
    = Cons(a,combine(l1,Cons(b,l2)))
```

88 It is good to start from a definition that covers all the cases.

```
fun combine(Empty,l2)
    = l2
  | combine(Cons(a,l1),l2)
    = Cons(a,combine(l1,l2))
```

What does *combine* consume and produce?

89 It consumes a pair of α *lists* and produces one.

```
combine :
  ((α list) * (α list)) → α list
```
•

What is the value of

```
combine(
  Cons(1,
    Cons(2,
      Cons(3,
        Empty))),
  Cons(5,
    Cons(4,
      Cons(7,
        Cons(9,
          Empty)))))?
```

90 That's no problem:

```
Cons(1,
  Cons(2,
    Cons(3,
      Cons(5,
        Cons(4,
          Cons(7,
            Cons(9,
              Empty))))))).
```

What is the value of

```
combine(
  Cons(1,
    Cons(2,
      Cons(3,
        Empty))),
  Cons(12,
    Cons(11,
      Cons(5,
        Cons(7,
          Empty)))))?
```

91 It starts with the same numbers:

```
Cons(1,
  Cons(2,
    Cons(3,
      Cons(12,
        Cons(11,
          Cons(5,
            Cons(7,
              Empty))))))).
```

Define *combine_c*.

92 That must be the function that consumes one list and produces a function that consumes a list and then produces the combined list.

Yes.

93 That's easy then.

```
fun combine_c(Empty)(l2)
    = l2
  | combine_c(Cons(a,l1))(l2)
    = Cons(a,combine_c(l1)(l2))
```

```
combine_c :
  α list → (α list → α list)
```

•

---

94 The stage is set. What is the value of

```
combine_c(
  Cons(1,
    Cons(2,
      Cons(3,
        Empty))))?
```

A function that consumes a list and prefixes that list with 1, 2, and 3.

---

95 Define a function that is like the value of

```
combine_c(
  Cons(1,
    Cons(2,
      Cons(3,
        Empty)))).
```

Easy.

```
fun prefixer_123(l2)
  = Cons(1,
      Cons(2,
        Cons(3,
          l2)))
```

```
prefixer_123 :
  int list → int list
```

---

96 It is an approximation.

Why?

---

97 When *prefixer_123* is used on a list, three Conses happen and nothing else. But when the value of

```
combine_c(
  Cons(1,
    Cons(2,
      Cons(3,
        Empty))))
```

is used, *combine_c* has only seen the first Cons.

Aha. Then here is an improvement.

```
fun waiting_prefix_123(l2)
  = Cons(1,
      combine_c(
        Cons(2,
          Cons(3,
            Empty)))
      (l2))
```

```
waiting_prefix_123 :
  int list → int list
```

---

98 Yes, *waiting_prefix_123* is "intensionally" more accurate than *prefixer_123*.

What does that mean?

99 The functions *waiting_prefix_123* and *prefixer_123* are "extensionally" equal because they produce the same values when they consume (extensionally) equal values.

Does "intensional" mean they differ in how they produce the values?

100 Exactly. Can we define a function like *combine_c* that produces *prefixer_123* when used with

```
Cons(1,
  Cons(2,
    Cons(3,
      Empty)))?
```

How could we do that?

101 The name *l2* must disappear from the definition. Define this new version, called *combine_s*.[1]

[1] A better name for this function would be `combine_staged`.

Here is a start.

```
fun combine_s(Empty)
  = ________
  | combine_s(Cons(a,l1))
  = ________
```

102 What does *combine_s* consume and produce?

It consumes an α *list* and produces a function from α *list* to α *list*:

α *list* $\rightarrow$ (α *list* $\rightarrow$ α *list*).

103 How must we fill in the first blank?

With a function that consumes a list, the former *l2*, and produces that very list.

104 Define this function.

Simple enough.

```
fun base(l2)
  = l2
```

```
base :
  α list → α list
```

105 Yes, and with that we can give a better definition.

```
fun combine_s(Empty)
    = base
  | combine_s(Cons(a,l1))
    = __________
```

Good, that leaves us with one blank.

---

106 What kind of answer do we need to fill the last blank?

Another function.

---

107 What does that function consume?

A list.

---

108 What does it produce?

A list that starts with *a*.

---

109 And what is the rest of the list?

The combination of *l1* and the new value.

---

110 Let's call the function that makes this function *make_cons* and let's use it to complete the definition of *combine_s*.

```
fun
    combine_s(Empty)
    = base
  | combine_s(Cons(a,l1))
    = make_cons(a,combine_s(l1))
and
    make_cons(a,f)
    = ...
                                  ⊗
```

Yes, that would do it.

---

111 What does *make_cons* consume to produce the function we want?

The definition tells us that it consumes a value of type α and a function with the same type as *base*.

Complete the definition of *make_cons*.

```
fun
    combine_s(Empty)
    = base
  | combine_s(Cons(a,l1))
    = make_cons(a,combine_s(l1))
and
    make_cons(a,f)(l2)
    = ________
```

112 One part is obvious.

```
fun
    combine_s(Empty)
    = base
  | combine_s(Cons(a,l1))
    = make_cons(a,combine_s(l1))
and
    make_cons(a,f)(l2)
    = Cons(a,________)
```

What does f consume?

113 An α *list*.

Is there one?

114 Yes, *l2* is an α *list*.

Go for it.

115 Oh that's good. Now we can complete it.

```
fun
    combine_s(Empty)
    = base
  | combine_s(Cons(a,l1))
    = make_cons(a,combine_s(l1))
and
    make_cons(a,f)(l2)
    = Cons(a,f(l2))
```

combine_s :
α *list* $\rightarrow$ (α *list* $\rightarrow$ α *list*) •

make_cons :
(α * (α *list* $\rightarrow$ α *list*))
$\rightarrow$
(α *list* $\rightarrow$ α *list*) •

116 What is the value of
combine_s(
Cons(1,
Cons(2,
Cons(3,
Empty))))?

It is equivalent to the value of
make_cons(1
make_cons(2,
make_cons(3,
base))).

---

117 What is the value of
make_cons(3,
base)?

It is this function.

```
fun prefix_3(l2)
    = Cons(3,base(l2))
```

```
prefix_3 :
  int list → int list
```

---

118 Then what is the value of
make_cons(2,
prefix_3)?

No big deal.

```
fun prefix_23(l2)
    = Cons(2,prefix_3(l2))
```

```
prefix_23 :
  int list → int list
```

---

119 So what is the value of
make_cons(1,
prefix_23)?

A function that consumes a list and prefixes that list with 1, 2, and 3.

```
fun prefix_123(l2)
    = Cons(1,prefix_23(l2))
```

```
prefix_123 :
  int list → int list
```

120 Is *prefix_123* equal to *prefixer_123*?

Extensionally, yes. Both prefix a list with 1, 2, and 3. Intensionally, no. The latter just Conses the numbers onto a list, but the former has to shuffle the list around with *make_cons*.

---

121 Can we define a function like *combine_s* that produces *prefixer_123* when used with

```
Cons(1,
  Cons(2,
    Cons(3,
      Empty)))?
```

We'd rather have dessert. How about you?

---

122 What is the difference between functions of type

$\mathbf{type}_1 \rightarrow \mathbf{type}_2 \rightarrow \mathbf{type}_3$

and those of type

$(\mathbf{type}_1 * \mathbf{type}_2) \rightarrow \mathbf{type}_3$?

Easy, they have different types.

---

123 Seriously.

The first kind of function consumes two values in two stages and may determine some aspect of the value it produces before it consumes the second value. The second kind of function consumes two values as a pair.

---

124 Aren't functions a lot of **fun**?

They sure are.

---

125 Rest up before continuing, unless you are exceptionally hungry.

See you tomorrow.

The Eighth Moral

Replace stars by arrows to reduce the number of values consumed and to increase the generality of the function defined.

9.
Oh No!

Did you ever play "Steal the Bacon?"

1 No, what about it?

We just invented "Find the Bacon."

2 How does it work?

We need to practice first.

3 What are we waiting for?

Lists.

4 Lists are easy, they have been done before.

```
datatype α list =
   Empty
 | Cons of α * α list
```

And we also use this datatype.

```
datatype box¹ =
   Bacon
 | Ix¹ of int
```

[1] Better names for these are `bacon_or_index` and `Index`, respectively.

5 There is some Bacon.

What is the value of

```
where_is(
  Cons(Ix(5),
    Cons(Ix(13),
      Cons(Bacon,
        Cons(Ix(8),
          Empty)))))?
```

6 3, right?

What is the value of

```
where_is(
  Cons(Bacon,
    Cons(Ix(8),
      Empty)))?
```

7 1, because Bacon is the first thing in the list.

What should be the value of
where_is(
  Cons(Ix(5),
    Cons(Ix(13),
      Cons(Ix(8),
        Empty))))?

8 0, because there is no Bacon in the list.

Here is the function *is_bacon*.

```
fun is_bacon(Bacon)
      = true
  | is_bacon(Ix(n))
      = false
```

```
is_bacon :
  box → bool
```

Use it to define *where_is*.

9 This shouldn't be a problem.

```
fun where_is(Empty)
      = 0
  | where_is(Cons(a_box,rest))
      = if is_bacon(a_box)
          then 1
          else 1 + where_is(rest)
```

```
where_is :
  box list → int
```

Use your definition to determine the value of
where_is(
  Cons(Ix(5),
    Cons(Ix(13),
      Cons(Ix(8),
        Empty)))).

10 Oh no. It's 3.

What were we expecting?

11 0, of course.

How did that happen?

12 When *where_is* produced 0, three additions were waiting for the result:

```
1 +
 1 +
  1 + ... .
```

We should forget these additions when we return 0, shouldn't we?

13 That would be great.

There is a way to do precisely that. Take a look at these definitions.

```
exception No_bacon of int
```

```
fun where_is(Empty)
      = raise No_bacon(0)
  | where_is(Cons(a_box,rest))
      = if is_bacon(a_box)
          then 1
          else 1 + where_is(rest)
```

14 They contain two new special words:

exception and **raise**.

Use your own words to describe what **exception** means.

15 You knew that we wouldn't let you down. Here are our words:

"The **exception** definition creates a constructor just like a **datatype** definition but for exceptional values. The expression No_bacon(10) creates such an exceptional value."

What does **raise** mean?

16 Can we just watch it in action?

Yes, let's slowly determine the value of

```
where_is(
  Cons(Ix(5),
    Cons(Ix(13),
      Cons(Ix(8),
        Empty)))).
```

17 Yes, let's do that.

Since the list is constructed with Cons, this is equal to

```
1 + where_is(
      Cons(Ix(13),
        Cons(Ix(8),
          Empty))).
```

18 Which in turn is equal to

```
1 +
  1 + where_is(
        Cons(Ix(8),
          Empty)).
```

Correct. And that is equal to

```
1 +
 1 +
  1 + where_is(
        Empty).
```

19 Now **raise** happens:

```
1 +
 1 +
  1 + raise No_bacon(0).
```

But what does that mean? Isn't it nonsense?

No,
because we can think of **raise** ... as having the *necessary* type, whatever it may be.

20 We have never seen anything like that before. Still, the answer does not explain what the expression means.

The meaning of **raise** ... is equally simple. It does not have a value.

21 It has no value? No wonder it has whatever type it needs to have. But that is strange.

So next we have

```
raise No_bacon(0).
```

Where did the additions go?

22 They've disappeared.

Good. Now we know that

```
where_is(
 Cons(Ix(5),
  Cons(Ix(13),
   Cons(Ix(8),
    Empty))))
```

has no value but is equal to

```
raise No_bacon(0).
```

23 Does that mean we didn't make any progress?

We made some progress. The additions are gone.

24 Yes, but we wanted an *int*; we wanted 0.

Don't worry, we will get there. Did you notice that we said *where_is* does not produce a value when it consumes a list without Bacon?

25 Yes, we said that.

But didn't we say that *where_is* produces an *int*?

26 Yes, but how can we say that it doesn't produce an *int* for everything that it consumes?

We can't. We just know that when we say *where_is* is of type

$(box\ list) \rightarrow int$,

we include the possibility that the function **raise**s an exception.

27 Aha, that clarifies it.

Is that all that bad?

28 It depends. If we only determine the value of

```
where_is(
  Cons(Ix(5),
    Cons(Ix(13),
      Cons(Ix(8),
        Empty)))),
```

we are just fine. If we get a number, we know that the list contains Bacon and where it is. If it **raise**s an exception, we know there is no Bacon.

How do we know when the function **raise**s an exception?

29 Good question.

We need yet another ingredient called **handle**.

30 And how do we use this new ingredient?

Like this:

```
(where_is(
   Cons(Ix(5),
     Cons(Ix(13),
       Cons(Ix(8),
         Empty))))
  handle
   No_bacon(an_int)
   ⇒[1] an_int).
```

[1] This is a two-character symbol: =>.

31 It seems like we are looking at a new form of expression:

$(exp_1$ **handle** $pattern \Rightarrow exp_2)$.

But what does it mean?

What do you think it means?

32 We know that the **handle** expression consumes exceptional values. So, when

```
where_is(
  Cons(Ix(5),
    Cons(Ix(13),
      Cons(Ix(8),
        Empty))))
```

is the same as

```
raise No_bacon(0),
```

it matches the **handle**r pattern and produces whatever is to the right of ⇒.

And how does No_bacon(0) match No_bacon(*an_int*)?

33 That's barely worth a question. It's certainly not worthy of an answer.

Let *an_int* stand for 0. Then what is the value in our example?

34 Exactly what we want: 0, which is what is to the right of ⇒ with *an_int* replaced by 0.

What is the value of

```
(where_is(
   Cons(Ix(5),
     Cons(Bacon,
       Cons(Ix(8),
         Empty))))
 handle
   No_bacon(an_int)
   => an_int)?
```

35 It is 2,
because Bacon is in the second position and no exception is **raise**d.

What kind of value does

```
(where_is(
  ...)
 handle
   No_bacon(an_int)
   => an_int)
```

produce if the value consumed contains Bacon?

36 An *int*.

And what if it doesn't contain Bacon? | 37 Also an *int*.

Does that mean that both parts of a **handle** expression must produce values of the same type? | 38 Yes, they must.

Have you seen anything like that before? | 39 Yes, the two branches of an **if**-expression must produce values that belong to the same type.

Ready to play the game? | 40 Yeah, we want to find the Bacon.

Here is a list with five *box*es:

```
Cons(Ix(5),
 Cons(Ix(4),
  Cons(Bacon,
   Cons(Ix(2),
    Cons(Ix(3),
     Empty))))).
```

Think of a number. Quick. | 41 1.

First, we check to see whether the 1st item is Bacon. If it is, we found it. | 42 Do we get to eat it?

No. If we found it, we just know where we found it. | 43 And if not?

Then, the 1st component must be Ix(i). | 44 The rest is obvious: We start the game over only this time with i, right?

Exactly. What is the value of

```
find(1,
  Cons(Ix(5),
    Cons(Ix(4),
      Cons(Bacon,
        Cons(Ix(2),
          Cons(Ix(3),
            Empty))))))?
```

45 According to our rules, the answer is 3.

And how do we get that answer?

46 We look at the first component, which is Ix(5).

Then we look at the fifth component.

47 Which is Ix(3) and the third component is Bacon.

Wasn't that easy?

48 Easy as quiche lorraine.

Then let's look for more bacon. What is the value of

```
find(2,
  Cons(Ix(5),
    Cons(Ix(4),
      Cons(Bacon,
        Cons(Ix(2),
          Cons(Ix(3),
            Empty))))))?
```

49 Well, we must check the second component, which is Ix(4).

And what is the fourth component?

50 It is Ix(2).

Weren't we just here?

51 Yes, we were.

Will we ever find the bacon?

52 We will never find Bacon.

Never?	53 Yes, we will just keep on looking at the second and the fourth components forever.
What kind of value does *find* consume?	54 It consumes a pair of an *int* and a *box list*: $(int * (box\ list))$.
And what kind of value does it produce?	55 It produces an *int*.
But didn't we just say that sometimes it doesn't produce a value?	56 Yes, but how can we say that?
We say that such uses of functions are meaningless.[1] [1] We use the word "meaningless" to refer to expressions for which nobody can determine a value.	57 Is meaningless like nonsense?
No, remember we can discover nonsense by just looking at the text of a function, but to discover that the use of a function is meaningless, we must try to determine the value.	58 Yes, they are obviously different. But how can we use types to warn others about meaningless functions?
We can't. We just know that when we say *find* is of type $(int * (box\ list)) \rightarrow int$ that we include the possibility that a use of *find* is meaningless.	59 Everything is clear now.
Didn't we just go through this discussion before?	60 Yes, we said the same thing about raising exceptions.

61 Put in your own words what it means to say some function f is of type

_____ $\rightarrow$ *out*.

We say:
"If f produces a value, that value is of type *out*. But, the use of f may be meaningless or it may **raise** an exception."

---

62 Does every function type have this extended meaning?

Absolutely.

---

63 Time to define *find*, isn't it?

Don't we need a function like *chain_item* for lists?

---

64 Good point. Define it.

Here is a part of it.

```
fun list_item(n,Empty)
    = ________
  | list_item(n,Cons(abox,rest))
    = if eq_int(n,1)
        then abox
        else list_item(n - 1,rest)
```

---

65 Why is the first answer a blank?

Because it is not clear what *list_item* produces when the list is empty.

---

66 Let's raise an exception. Here is its definition.

```
exception Out_of_range
```

Well, then it is easy to fill in the blank.

```
fun list_item(n,Empty)
    = raise Out_of_range
  | list_item(n,Cons(abox,rest))
    = if eq_int(n,1)
        then abox
        else list_item(n - 1,rest)
```

```
list_item :
  (int * box list) → box
```

67 Does this definition differ from anything we have seen before?

```
fun
    find(n,boxes)
    = check(n,boxes,list_item(n,boxes))
and
    check(n,boxes,Bacon)
    = n
  | check(n,boxes,Ix(i))
    = find(i,boxes)
```

```
find :
  (int * (box list)) → int
```

```
check :
  (int * (box list) * box) → int
```

Very.

---

68 That's correct. Does the definition of *box* refer to itself?

No.

---

69 Does the definition of *find* refer to itself?

Yes, through *check*.

---

70 Isn't that unusual?

We have not seen that combination before.

---

71 Does that mean the definition of *find* matches neither the outline of the datatype *box* nor that of the datatype *box list*?

That's right, it doesn't.

---

72 Then what is the reference to *find* used for?

It is used to restart the search for Bacon with a new index.

---

73 Isn't this unusual?

Very.

And that kind of reference is precisely why a use of *find* may be meaningless.

74 That settles it.

What is the value of

find(1,*t*)

where *t* is

```
Cons(Ix(5),
  Cons(Ix(4),
    Cons(Bacon,
      Cons(Ix(2),
        Cons(Ix(7),
          Empty)))))?
```

75 Is *t* going to change?[1]

[1] We can write

```
val t =
    Cons(Ix(5),
      Cons(Ix(4),
        Cons(Bacon,
          Cons(Ix(2),
            Cons(Ix(7),
              Empty)))))
```

in order to associate the name *t* with this value.

No, it will stay the same for the rest of the chapter. So what is the value?

76 The expression is the same as the value of

find(5,*t*).

And then?

77 Then it is the same as *find*(7,*t*).

And now?

78 An exception is raised.

And what does that mean?

79 Every time *find* raises an exception, the bacon can't be found.

Let's try something new. We will restart the search at *n* div 2.

80 What does that mean?

What is the value of 8 div 2?

81 Obvious: 4.

What is the value of 7 div 2?

82 Not so obvious: 3.

How can we restart the search when the number is out of range?

83 We can use a **handler**.

Good. Fill in the blank.

```
fun find(n,boxes)
    = (check(n,boxes,list_item(n,boxes))
        handle
        Out_of_range
        ⇒ __________ )
and
    check(n,boxes,Bacon)
    = n
  | check(n,boxes,Ix(i))
    = find(i,boxes)
```

84 Okay.

```
fun find(n,boxes)
    = (check(n,boxes,list_item(n,boxes))
        handle
        Out_of_range
        ⇒ find(n div 2,boxes))
and
    check(n,boxes,Bacon)
    = n
  | check(n,boxes,Ix(i))
    = find(i,boxes)
```

```
find :
  (int * (box list)) → int
```

```
check :
  (int * (box list) * box) → int
```

Now the plot really thickens.

85 Like pea soup?

Now what is the value of
find(1,*t*)?

86 It is the same as the value of

```
(find(5,t)
 handle
 Out_of_range
 ⇒ find(1 div 2,t)).
```

And then?

87 Then it is the same as

```
((find(7,t)
  handle
  Out_of_range
  ⇒ find(5 div 2,t))
 handle
 Out_of_range
 ⇒ find(1 div 2,t)).
```

And now?

88 The next stop is

```
(((check(7,t,list_item(7,t))
    handle
    Out_of_range
    ⇒ find(7 div 2,t))
   handle
   Out_of_range
   ⇒ find(5 div 2,t))
  handle
  Out_of_range
  ⇒ find(1 div 2,t)).
```

And here *list_item*(7,*t*) raises an exception.

What does that mean?

89 It means *list_item*(7,*t*) doesn't have a value but is equal to **raise** Out_of_range, so that we get

```
(((check(7,t,raise Out_of_range)
    handle
    Out_of_range
    ⇒ find(7 div 2,t))
   handle
   Out_of_range
   ⇒ find(5 div 2,t))
  handle
  Out_of_range
  ⇒ find(1 div 2,t)).
```

Does *check*(7,*t*,...) disappear, too?

90 Yes, **raise** does that.

How is the exception **handle**d then?

91 By matching with Out_of_range.

Yes, and then we evaluate *find*(7 div 2,*t*). What is the next expression?

92 Easy:

```
((find(3,t)
   handle
   Out_of_range
   ⇒ find(5 div 2,t))
  handle
  Out_of_range
  ⇒ find(1 div 2,t)).
```

Next?

93 We have found the Bacon, which means the result is 3.

Where have the **handle**rs gone?

94 Since *find*(3,*t*) has a value, the **handle**rs disappear.

Where did we stop while we were searching for the bacon?

95 At 1, 5, 7, and 3.

Could we define a function that produces that sequence for us?

96 Yes, as an *int list*.

Hang on!

97 Is it going to get more complicated still?

Yes! Look at this definition of *path*.

```
fun path(n,boxes)
    = Cons(n,
        (check(n,boxes,list_item(n,boxes))
         handle
         Out_of_range
         => path(n div 2,boxes)))
and
    check(n,boxes,Bacon)
    = Empty
  | check(n,boxes,Ix(i))
    = path(i,boxes)
```

```
path :
  (int * (box list)) -> (int list)
```

```
check :
  (int * (box list) * box) -> (int list)
```

Do we still need to have *n* around in *check*?

98 No, that much is obvious.

```
fun path(n,boxes)
    = Cons(n,
        (check(boxes,list_item(n,boxes))
         handle
         Out_of_range
         => path(n div 2,boxes)))
and
    check(boxes,Bacon)
    = Empty
  | check(boxes,Ix(i))
    = path(i,boxes)
```

```
path :
  (int * (box list)) -> (int list)
```

```
check :
  ((box list) * box) -> (int list)
```

Describe in your own words how this function produces the list of intermediate stops.

99 What?

Neither can we. So let's just determine the value of

path(1,*t*).

100 Well, *list_item* produces Ix(5), which means that it is equal to

```
Cons(1,
  (path(5,t)
   handle
   Out_of_range
   ⇒ path(1 div 2,t))).
```

And then?

101 Then it is the same as

```
Cons(1,
  (Cons(5,
     (path(7,t)
      handle
      Out_of_range
      ⇒ path(5 div 2,t)))
   handle
   Out_of_range
   ⇒ path(1 div 2,t))).
```

And the next stop is

```
Cons(1,
  (Cons(5,
     (Cons(7,
        ((check(t,list_item(7,t))
          handle
          Out_of_range
          ⇒ path(7 div 2,t))))
      handle
      Out_of_range
      ⇒ path(5 div 2,t)))
    handle
    Out_of_range
    ⇒ path(1 div 2,t))).
```

Here *list_item*(7,*t*) raises an exception.

102 Right and we get

```
Cons(1,
  (Cons(5,
     (Cons(7,
        ((check(t,raise Out_of_range)
          handle
          Out_of_range
          ⇒ path(7 div 2,t))))
      handle
      Out_of_range
      ⇒ path(5 div 2,t)))
    handle
    Out_of_range
    ⇒ path(1 div 2,t))).
```

Does this **raise** also make *check*$(t, \ldots)$ disappear?	103 Yes, it, too, disappears.
How is the exception **handle**d?	104 By matching with Out_of_range and evaluating *path*(7 div 2,*t*) next.
So what is our next expression?	105 Easy:

```
Cons(1,
  (Cons(5,
   (Cons(7,
      path(3,t))
    handle
    Out_of_range
    ⇒ path(5 div 2,t)))
   handle
   Out_of_range
   ⇒ path(1 div 2,t))).
```

Next?	106 We have found the Bacon:

```
Cons(1,
  Cons(5,
    Cons(7,
      Cons(3,
        Empty)))).
```

Where have all the **handle**rs gone?	107 Since *path*(3,*t*) has a value, the **handle**rs disappear.
Is this an exceptional journey?	108 Quite, and it sure makes us hungry.

The Ninth Moral

Some functions produce exceptions instead of values; some don't produce anything. Handle raised exceptions carefully.

10. Building On Blocks

What is the value of *plus*(0,1)?

1 1. But isn't that obvious?

Yes, it's obvious, so let's move on. What is the value of *plus*(1,1)?

2 2, which is also one more than *plus*(0,1).

Correct. Here is the final question. What is the value of *plus*(2,1)?

3 3, which is one more than *plus*(1,1).

Here is a definition of *plus* based on the previous questions.

```
fun plus(n,m)
    = if is_zero(n)
        then m
        else succ(plus(pred(n),m))
```

```
plus :
  (int * int) → int
```

It relies on three help functions: *is_zero*, *pred*, and *succ*.[1] Define these help functions.

[1] Better names for these functions are `predecessor` and `successor`, respectively.

4 They are easy functions.

```
fun is_zero(n)
    = eq_int(n,0)
```

```
is_zero :
  int → bool
```

```
exception Too_small
```

```
fun pred(n)
    = if eq_int(n,0)
        then raise Too_small
        else n - 1
```

```
pred :
  int → int
```

```
fun succ(n)
    = n + 1
```

```
succ :
  int → int
```

Why does *pred* raise an exception when it consumes 0?

5 We only work with non-negative *ints*, so 0 does not have a predecessor.

Define the function *plus* in the same style, but use *nums* in place of *ints*.

```
datatype num =
   Zero
 | One_more_than of num
```

Here are the help functions that we need.

```
fun is_zero(Zero)
    = true
  | is_zero(not_zero)
    = false
```

```
is_zero :
  num → bool                                   •
```

```
exception Too_small
```

```
fun pred(Zero)
    = raise Too_small
  | pred(One_more_than(n))
    = n
```

```
pred :
  num → num                                    •
```

```
fun succ(n)
    = One_more_than(n)
```

```
succ :
  num → num                                    •
```

6 With those, it is a piece of cake.

```
fun plus(n,m)
    = if is_zero(n)
        then m
        else succ(plus(pred(n),m))
```

```
plus :
  (num * num) → num                            •
```

Isn't it curious that the two definitions of *plus* are identical?

7 Yes, and that's good.

Why?

8 Because the functions are closely related. They produce similar values when they consume similar pairs of values.

What is the value of

plus(2,3)?

9 This is nonsense. The last definition of *plus* consumes a pair of *nums* and produces one. It cannot be used with *ints*.

What is the value of

```
plus(
  One_more_than(
    One_more_than(
      Zero)),
  One_more_than(
    One_more_than(
      One_more_than(
        Zero))))?
```

10 Now we are making sense. It is

```
One_more_than(
  One_more_than(
    One_more_than(
      One_more_than(
        One_more_than(
          Zero))))).
```

Isn't it unfortunate that we can't use the two versions of *plus* at the same time?

11 It truly is. But because the two definitions are identical, we must use building blocks with the same names, even though they consume and produce values of different types.

Any ideas about what to do?

12 There seems to be no other way to do this. For each definition of *plus* we need to have around the two sets of building blocks. Each set requires definitions for the same set of names. Because it is impossible to use a name for two different definitions, we cannot have two definitions of *plus* available at the same time.

There is a way and we are about to discover it.

13 Oh great.

What are the basic building blocks needed to make *plus*?

14 There are five:
the type,
the exception Too_small,
the function *succ*,
the function *pred*,
and
the function *is_zero*.

If we call the type *number*, what is the type of the building block *succ*?

15 The type of *succ* is
$number \to number$.

And how about *pred*?

16 It has the same type:
$number \to number$.

And *is_zero*?

17 It produces a *bool*:
$number \to bool$.

Good, and here is a way to write down these minimal requirements for our building blocks.

```
signature N[1] =
  sig
    type number
    exception Too_small
    val succ : number → number
    val pred : number → number
    val is_zero : number → bool
  end
```

[1] A better name for this signature would be NUMBERS_BY_PEANO.

18 This is clear enough. This notation specifies five things between **sig** and **end**, but what do **signature**, **type**, and **val** mean?

The word **signature** makes a name stand for a signature. Our example defines the name N. The signature is the collection of things listed between **sig** and **end**.	19	That much makes sense.
The word **type** in between **sig** ... **end** indicates that *number* is used as the name of a type.	20	Do we know anything else about the type?
Not much. All we know here is that the type is used to describe what the **val**ues *succ*, *pred*, and *is_zero* consume and produce.	21	Now that explains **val** in signatures. The word **val** says that we must have values of a certain kind. In our example all three values are functions over *number*s.
What is a signature?	22	We have seen a signature, but we don't yet know what it is.
A signature is like a type $int \rightarrow int$. Each element of this type must be a function, and furthermore, each element must consume and produce an *int*.	23	Well, we know what the elements of a type like $int \rightarrow int$ are, but what are the elements of a signature?
The elements are called structures but we don't usually call them elements. We say that a structure has a signature.	24	What does a signature say about a structure?
A signature describes the components of structures. Before we can say that a structure has some signature, we must check that it provides all the required pieces.	25	Fair enough. Before we say that some function f has the type $int \rightarrow int$ we check that it consumes and produces *int*s. But have we seen structures yet?

Not yet. We produce structures with **functor**, (,), and **struct** ... **end**. Here is one for *nums*; create one for *ints*.

```
functor NumberAsNum()
  ▷
  N
  =
  struct
    datatype num =
      Zero
     | One_more_than of num
    type number = num
    exception Too_small
    fun succ(n)
        = One_more_than(n)
    fun pred(Zero)
        = raise Too_small
      | pred(One_more_than(n))
        = n
    fun is_zero(Zero)
        = true
      | is_zero(a_num)
        = false
  end
```

26 The structure for *ints* must also contain the required basic building blocks.

```
functor NumberAsInt()
  ▷[1]
  N
  =
  struct
    type number = int
    exception Too_small
    fun succ(n)
        = n + 1
    fun pred(n)
        = if eq_int(n,0)
            then raise Too_small
            else n - 1
    fun is_zero(n)
        = eq_int(n,0)
  end
```

This notation defines several things between **struct** and **end**. We already know that **fun** defines functions, **datatype** creates a new type, but what does **type** mean here?

[1] This is a two-character symbol :>.

The words
  type *number* = ...
in
  struct ... **end**
indicate that *number* stands for whatever is to the right of =.

27 So that is how we know that in the first example *numbers* are made from *nums* and in the second one from *ints*. But what do **functor**, (), and ▷ mean?

The word **functor** makes a name stand for something that produces structures. We refer to this thing as "functor." The first example introduces *NumberAsNum* as a functor's name, the second one *NumberAsInt*. Using the functor produces a structure that consists of the collection of definitions enclosed in **struct** ... **end**.

28 That much makes sense.

What does () mean?

29 Here are our words:
"It means that we are *defining* a functor that does not depend on anything else."

Good. We will see things other than ().

30 Okay, and then the meaning of "depend" should become clearer.

So what is the notation ... $\triangleright$ N about?

31 It states that the result of using the functor is a structure with signature N.

Do both of these functors produce structures that have the signature N?

32 Each **struct** ... **end** contains several definitions, but at least one for *number*, Too_small, *succ*, *pred*, and *is_zero*. And, in terms of *number*, the three **val**ues have the right type.

Now let's use a functor to build a structure.

```
structure IntStruct =
  NumberAsInt()
```

What is the signature of *IntStruct*?

33 It is N obviously, because the definition of *NumberAsInt* states that the functor produces structures with signature N.

And what does () behind *NumberAsInt* mean?

34 Here are our words:
"It means that we are *using* a functor that does not depend on anything else."

Define the structure *NumStruct*.

35 That's obvious now.

```
structure NumStruct =
  NumberAsNum()
```

Why are we doing all of this?

36 Is it because we want to use both versions of *plus* at the same time and, if possible, create them from the same text?

Do we now have both sets of building blocks around at the same time?

37 Basically. Those for *nums* are collected in *NumStruct* and those for *ints* in *IntStruct*.

Is this progress?

38 Yes, if we can now somehow create the two versions of *plus* from the two structures.

Exactly. What is the type of *plus*?

39 If *number* is the type, then *plus* has the type

(*number* ∗ *number*) → *number*.

Define a signature that says that.

40 Here is one.

```
signature P¹ =
  sig
    type number
    val plus :
          (number * number) → number
  end
```

[1] A better name for this signature would be PLUS_OVER_NUMBER.

Here is the functor.

```
functor PON¹(structure a_N : N)
  ▷
  P
  =
  struct
    type number = a_N.number
    fun plus(n,m)
       = if a_N.is_zero(n)
           then m
           else a_N.succ(
                  plus(a_N.pred(n),m))
  end
```

How does it differ from the functors we have seen so far?

[1] A better name for this functor would be PlusOverNumber.

41 The names of the other functors are always followed by (). This one, however, contains something else:

(**structure** *a_N* : *N*).

What does it mean?

The notation

(**structure** *a_N* : *N*)

says that the structure produced by *PON* depends on a structure *a_N* that has signature *N*.

42 And that's how we know that *a_N* contains a type, an exception, and three values: *is_zero*, *succ*, and *pred*.

What does *a_N.is_zero* mean?

43 It means that we are using the **val**ue named *is_zero* from the structure named *a_N*.

Correct. And how about

a_N.number,

a_N.succ,

and

a_N.pred?

44 They refer to

a_N's **type** *number*,

a_N's **val**ue *succ*,

and

a_N's **val**ue *pred*,

respectively.

And how do we know that *a_N* contains all these things?

45 Because it has signature *N*.

Let's build a structure from *PON*.

46 We don't know how to satisfy *PON*'s dependency.

We need a new notation.

```
structure IntArith =
  PON(structure a_N = IntStruct)
```

47 Yet more notation?

Yes. Explain in your words what it means.

48 Our words:

"Consider the functor's dependency:

(**structure** *a_N* : *N*).

It specifies that the structure created by *PON* depends on a yet to be determined structure *a_N* with signature *N*. Here we say that *a_N* stands for *IntStruct*."

Does *IntStruct* have the signature *N*?	49 The structure was created with *NumberAsInt*, which always produces structures that have signature *N*.
And how do we know that?	50 The definition of *NumberAsInt* contains *N* below ▷, and that's what says the resulting structure has signature *N*.
Time to create *plus* over *nums*.	51 Easy. **structure** *NumArith* = *PON*(**structure** *a_N* = *NumStruct*)
What is the value of *IntArith.plus*(1,2)?	52 This should be 3.
Wrong.	53 What! Nonsense!
Good guess! It is nonsense. What do we know about *IntArith*?	54 We know that it is a structure that has signature *P*.
What do we know about structures that have signature *P*?	55 A structure with signature *P* has two components: a type named *number* and a value named *plus*. The value *plus* consumes a pair of *numbers* and produces one.
And what else do we know about *number* in *P*?	56 Nothing, because the signature *P* does not reveal anything else about the structures that *PON* produces.
Absolutely. And that's why it is nonsense to ask for the value of *IntArith.plus*(1,2).	57 Okay, that's clear. The function *IntArith.plus* consumes values of type *IntArith.number*, about which *P* doesn't reveal anything, but 1 and 2 are *ints*.

Can we determine the value of
NumArith.plus(
One_more_than(Zero),
One_more_than(
One_more_than(Zero)))?

58 No. The function *NumArith.plus* consumes values of type *NumArith.number*, but

One_more_than(Zero)

and

One_more_than(
One_more_than(Zero))

are *nums*.

Do we have the means to produce *numbers* of the correct type for either *IntArith.plus* or *NumArith.plus*?

59 No, the two structures contain only one function, *plus*, and it assumes that we have *numbers* ready for consumption.

How about the structures *IntStruct* and *NumStruct*?

60 They, too, provide only functions that consume existing *numbers*.

So what do we do?

61 Yes, what?

Here is one way out. Let's use a larger signature.

```
signature N_C_R =
  sig
    type number
    exception Too_small
    val conceal : int → number
    val succ : number → number
    val pred : number → number
    val is_zero : number → bool
    val reveal : number → int
  end
```

62 The signature *N_C_R*[1] requires that its corresponding structures contain definitions for two additional functions: *conceal* and *reveal*. What can they be about?

[1] A better name for this signature would be NUMBERS_WITH_CONCEAL_REVEAL.

The function *conceal* consumes an *int* and produces a similar *number*.

63 Does *reveal* do the opposite?

Yes, and opposite means that for any *int* $x \geq 0$,

$reveal(conceal(x)) = x.$

64 Oh, *conceal* is like $(\cdot)^2$ (square) and *reveal* like $\sqrt{\cdot}$ (square root) because for any *int* $x \geq 0$,

$\sqrt{x^2} = x.$

Good. Here is the extended version of *NumberAsInt.*

```
functor NumberAsInt()
  ▷
  N_C_R
  =
  struct
    type number = int
    exception Too_small
    fun conceal(n)
        = n
    fun succ(n)
        = n + 1
    fun pred(n)
        = if eq_int(n,0)
             then raise Too_small
             else n - 1
    fun is_zero(n)
        = eq_int(n,0)
    fun reveal(n)
        = n
  end
```

Define the extended version of *NumberAsNum.*

65 That requires a bit more thought.

```
functor NumberAsNum()
  ▷
  N_C_R
  =
  struct
    datatype num =
        Zero
      | One_more_than of num
    type number = num
    exception Too_small
    fun conceal(n)
          = if eq_int(n,0)
               then Zero
               else One_more_than(
                      conceal(n - 1))
    fun succ(n)
          = One_more_than(n)
    fun pred(Zero)
          = raise Too_small
      | pred(One_more_than(n))
          = n
    fun is_zero(Zero)
          = true
      | is_zero(a_num)
          = false
    fun reveal(n)
          = if is_zero(n)
               then 0
               else 1 + reveal(pred(n))
  end
```

Let's rebuild the structures *IntStruct* and *IntArith*.

```
structure IntStruct =
  NumberAsInt()
```

```
structure IntArith =
  PON(structure a_N = IntStruct)
```

66 Okay, here are the new versions of *NumStruct* and *NumArith*.

```
structure NumStruct =
  NumberAsNum()
```

```
structure NumArith =
  PON(structure a_N = NumStruct)
```

What kind of structures are *IntStruct* and *NumStruct*?

67 Both have signature *N_C_R*.

What kind of structure does *PON* depend on?

68 It depends on a structure with signature *N*. Isn't this a conflict?

Does a structure with signature *N_C_R* provide all the things that a structure with signature *N* provides?

69 It does, and *N_C_R* even lists those pieces that are also in *N* in the same order as *N*.

Absolutely. And that's why it is okay to supply *IntStruct* and *NumStruct* to *PON*.

70 Okay.

What is the value of

```
NumStruct.reveal(
  NumStruct.succ(
    NumStruct.conceal(0)))?
```

71 1,
because *NumStruct.conceal* consumes an *int* and produces a *number* for the consumption of *NumStruct.succ*. And *NumStruct.reveal* consumes a *number* and produces an *int*.

What is the value of

```
NumStruct.reveal(
  NumArith.plus(
    NumStruct.conceal(1),
    NumStruct.conceal(2)))?
```

72 This should be 3, now.

Wrong.

73 What! Is that nonsense again?

Good guess! It is nonsense but this time it is "signature nonsense." What do we know about *NumArith*?

74 We know that it has signature *P*.

What do we know about structures with signature *P*?

75 A structure with signature *P* has two components: a type named *number* and a value named *plus*. The value *plus* consumes a pair of *number*s and produces one.

And what else do we know about *number* in *P*?

76 Nothing!

What do we know about structures with signature *N_C_R*?

77 They contain a type, also named *number*, an exception and five functions over *int* and *number*. The function *conceal* creates a *number* from an *int*, and *reveal* translates the *number* back into an *int*.

Do we know anything else about *number* in *N_C_R*?

78 Nothing, because the signature *N_C_R* does not reveal anything else about the structure.

So, how could we possibly know from just looking at the signatures alone that *NumStruct.conceal* produces the same kind of *number*s that *NumArith.plus* consumes?

79 From the signatures alone, we cannot know that the two kinds of *number*s are the same. Indeed, we could have used two different names for these types, like *number1* and *number2*. But why does that matter?

Because we must be able to determine from the signatures, and from the signatures only, that the type of an expression makes sense. If we cannot, the expression is nonsense.

80 This is analogous to expressions and types, except that now we relate types and signatures.

Are there other forms of signature nonsense?

81 Here is one:

NumStruct.Zero.

The signature doesn't say anything about a constructor Zero, so we can't know anything about it either.

Correct.

82 What shall we do?

We need to say that *PON* produces structures whose type *number* is the same as the type *number* in *a_N*, the functor's dependency.

83 And how do we do that?

We connect the signature of the structure produced by *PON* to the structure on which it depends.

```
functor PON(structure a_N : N)
  ▷
  P where type number = a_N.number
  =
  struct
   type number = a_N.number
   fun plus(n,m)
      = if a_N.is_zero(n)
          then m
          else a_N.succ(
                 plus(a_N.pred(n),m))
  end
```

84 Is

P **where type** *number* = *a_N.number*

a signature?

Yes, it is a signature and therefore can be used below ▷. A **where**-clause refines what a signature stands for.

85 So here, the signature is like *P* but requires that *number* in the functor's result must be equal to *a_N.number*.

And how do we make sure in **struct** ... **end** that this is the case?

86 We define the type *number* to be the type *number* of the structure *a_N*'s type *number*.

Do the two similar looking lines always go together?

87 For us, they do. One makes promises and the other fulfills the promises.

Let's create *plus* over *nums*.

structure *NumArith* =
  PON(**structure** *a_N* = *NumStruct*)

Is it different?

88 No, and the one for *IntArith* doesn't change either.

structure *IntArith* =
  PON(**structure** *a_N* = *IntStruct*)

What is the value of
  NumStruct.reveal(
    NumArith.plus(
      NumStruct.conceal(1),
      NumStruct.conceal(2)))?

89 3, because now it makes sense.

Can we also calculate with *ints*?

90 Can't we just replace *Num* by *Int* like this:
  IntStruct.reveal(
    IntArith.plus(
      IntStruct.conceal(1),
      IntStruct.conceal(2)))?

How about lunch?

91 I can't put the book down. How can you guys stop now?

Are you fortified?

92 Yes!

Then here is a second way out.

```
functor NumberAsInt2()
  ▷
  N where type number = int
  =
  struct
    type number = int
    exception Too_small
    fun succ(n)
        = n + 1
    fun pred(n)
        = if eq_int(n,0)
              then raise Too_small
              else n - 1
    fun is_zero(n)
        = eq_int(n,0)
  end
```

93 Out of what?

Out of the dilemma that we don't have anything that *PON*'s *plus* can consume.

94 Oh yes. We said that enlarging the signature for the basic building blocks was one way out. How does it help to add

where type *number* = *int*

to *N*, now?

Here is yet another definition of *IntStruct*.

```
structure IntStruct2 =
  NumberAsInt2()
```

What do we know about the signature of this structure?

95 It is like *N*, but we also know that the *numbers* are *ints*.

Yes. Now take a look at this definition of *IntArith2*.

```
structure IntArith2 =
  PON(structure a_N = IntStruct2)
```

What do we know about its signature?

96 We know that it's like *P* and that its *numbers* are *a_N*'s *numbers*.

And what are *a_N*'s *numbers*?	97	Since *a_N* is *IntStruct2*, we know from its signature that the *numbers* are *ints*.
So, if *IntArith2*'s *numbers* are those of *IntStruct2*, and if *IntStruct2*'s *numbers* are *ints*, what do we know?	98	We know that *IntArith2*'s *numbers* are *ints*.

What is the value of
  IntArith2.plus(
    1,
    2)?
	99	3.

Yes, it is.	100	That really helps.

How can we do something like
  NumArith2.plus(
    One_more_than(Zero),
    One_more_than(
      One_more_than(Zero)))?
	101	Well, we would have to define the structure *NumArith2*.

And what does it rely on?	102	To use it, we need the structure *NumStruct2*, which in turn is created from *NumberAsNum2*, a functor that reveals a lot about the structure that it produces.

103

Good. Here is the new functor.

```
functor NumberAsNum2()
  ▷
  N where type number = num
  =
  struct
    datatype num =
        Zero
      | One_more_than of num
    type number = num
    exception Too_small
    fun succ(n)
        = One_more_than(n)
    fun pred(Zero)
        = raise Too_small
      | pred(One_more_than(n))
        = n
    fun is_zero(Zero)
        = true
      | is_zero(a_num)
        = false
  end
                                        ⊗
```

If it weren't for ⊗, which says that this is nonsense, these would be *NumStruct2* and *NumArith2*.

```
structure NumStruct2 =
  NumberAsNum2()
                                        ⊗
```

```
structure NumArith2 =
  PON(structure a_N = NumStruct2)
                                        ⊗
```

104

Good guess, and indeed, it is nonsense.

But why is it nonsense?

105

Remember everything in **struct** ... **end** is invisible, and it is the signature that makes it public.

So if *num* in

where type *number* = *num*

does not refer to the datatype definition, to what does it refer then?

106

The word *num* in the above **where** clause refers to the **datatype** that we defined at the beginning of this chapter.

But the two definitions look so much alike!

The two definitions look the same, but they introduce two different types. In general, every **datatype** definition introduces a new type that is distinct from every other type.

107 That's an aspect of **datatype** we haven't discussed yet, isn't it?

True. There hasn't been a reason to discuss what two look-alike **datatype** definitions mean.

108 Could we get things right by removing the **datatype** definition for *num* from the functor? Then the functor definition, including its modified signature could only refer to the definition from the beginning of the chapter.

Yes we could, but we will save that for another book. Do you need more lunch before we move on?

109 An apple will be enough.

Is Zero the same as 0?

110 No, 0 is similar to, but not really the same as, Zero.

Is

```
One_more_than(
  One_more_than(
    Zero))
```

similar to

```
2?
```

111 Yes, 2 is similar to, but not the same as,

```
One_more_than(
  One_more_than(
    Zero)).
```

Define the function *similar*.

112 Should it only consume *nums* and *ints*?

No, it should work for any two structures that have the signature *N*.

113 That is more interesting.

Here is the signature for the functor that produces a structure containing *similar*.

```
signature S =
 sig
  type number1
  type number2
  val similar :
         (number1 * number2) → bool
 end
```

114 Okay, this is straightforward. A structure with signature S contains two types: *number1* and *number2*. It also contains a **val**ue *similar*, which consumes a pair consisting of *number1* and *number2* and produces true or false.

Does this functor differ from previous ones?

```
functor Same(structure a_N : N
             structure b_N : N)
 ▷
 S where type number1 = a_N.number
   where type number2 = b_N.number
 =
 struct
  type number1 = a_N.number
  type number2 = b_N.number
  fun sim(n,m)
      = if a_N.is_zero(n)
          then b_N.is_zero(m)
          else sim(a_N.pred(n),
                 b_N.pred(m))
  fun similar(n,m)
      = ((sim(n,m)
           handle
           a_N.Too_small ⇒ false)
          handle
          b_N.Too_small ⇒ false)
 end
```

115 Yes, this one depends on two structures, each of which has the signature N.

Are the **where** refinements of S necessary?

116 Yes, if we ever want to use *similar*.

How can we use *similar*?

117 Since the function can consume *numbers* produced by *a_N.conceal* and *b_N.conceal*, respectively, we just feed *similar numbers* produced with the proper *conceal* functions.

So let's create a structure that compares *nums* and *ints*.

118 The functor must consume two structures, and we already have the ones we need.

```
structure SimIntNum =
  Same(structure a_N = IntStruct
       structure b_N = NumStruct)
```

Is there another way to do it?

119 It's just a guess.

```
structure SimNumInt =
  Same(structure a_N = NumStruct
       structure b_N = IntStruct)
```

Good guess. Why?

120 Here is what we would have said:
"Because we supply one structure for each of the functor's dependencies."

Are functors like functions?

121 Yes, but they only consume and produce structures, not values.

What is the value of
SimNumInt.similar(
NumStruct.conceal(0),
IntStruct.conceal(0))?

122 true.

What is the value of
SimIntNum.similar(
IntStruct.conceal(0),
NumStruct.conceal(1))?

123 false.

124 We can also compare *nums* to *nums*.

```
structure SimNumNum =
  Same(structure a_N = NumStruct
       structure b_N = NumStruct)
```

How neat.

---

125 Is there a simpler way to define *similar*?

Yes, there is, but we would not have learned as much from that one, so we chose not to *reveal* it.

---

126 Isn't it snack time yet?

This should be our last break.

---

127 Here is a new function.

```
fun new_plus(x,y)
    = NumStruct.reveal(
        NumArith.plus(
          NumStruct.conceal(x),
          NumStruct.conceal(y)))
```

It's just addition, but it uses *nums*. We could have another one that uses *ints*.

```
fun new_plus(x,y)
    = IntStruct.reveal(
        IntArith.plus(
          IntStruct.conceal(x),
          IntStruct.conceal(y)))
```

---

128 Use your words to describe what *new_plus* does.

In our words:
"The function *new_plus* consumes two *ints*, converts them into one of our favorite number systems, adds them, and converts them back to *int*."

Here is a signature.

```
signature J =
  sig
    val new_plus : (int * int) → int
  end
```

129 It looks okay. It seems to consume a structure that has signature *N_C_R* and another one with signature *P*. The structure that it produces seems to have signature *J*.

And here is the functor *NP*.

```
functor NP(structure a_N : N_C_R
           structure a_P : P)
  ▷
  J
  =
  struct
    fun new_plus(x,y)
      = a_N.reveal(
          a_P.plus(
            a_N.conceal(x),
            a_N.conceal(y)))
  end                                   ⊗
```

Why is this definition nonsense?

Still, it is nonsense.

130 Why oh why?

Suppose we use this functor with *nums* and *IntArith*.

```
structure NP1 =
  NP(structure a_N = NumStruct
     structure a_P = IntArith)          ⊗
```

131 Now it's obvious why the definition of the functor is nonsense.

And that is?

132 The function *NumStruct.conceal* would produce numbers as *nums* and *IntArith.plus* would attempt to consume those, which is nonsense.

Why is it nonsense?

133 Because *IntArith.plus* consumes *ints*.

So what should we do?

134 We must force *a_N* and *a_P* to use the same kind of numbers.

That is perfect. And we do this by specifying that the types *a_N.number* and *a_P.number* must be the same.

```
functor NP[1](structure a_N : N_C_R
              structure a_P : P
              sharing type
                a_N.number
                =
                a_P.number)
  ▷
  J
  =
  struct
    fun new_plus(x,y)
        = a_N.reveal(
            a_P.plus(
              a_N.conceal(x),
              a_N.conceal(y)))
  end
```

Define a structure for adding *ints* using *nums*.

1 A better name for *NP* is `NewPlusFunctor`.

135 We just use *NP* with *NumStruct* and *NumArith*. That's all.

```
structure NPStruct =
  NP(structure a_N = NumStruct
     structure a_P = NumArith)
```

How do we know from the signatures that the type *number* in *NumStruct* is the same as the type *number* in *NumArith*?

136 The functor that creates *NumArith* is defined to produce structures that have signature

P **where type** *number* = *a_N.number*.

And what is *a_N.number* in our case?

137 We know that we create *NumArith* from *PON* with *NumStruct*. And therefore the type *number* in *NumStruct* and the type *number* in *NumArith* are equal.

Does that mean the sharing constraint is satisfied?

138 Yes.

Can we say all that in one expression?

139 That would be nice. We wouldn't have to turn so many pages.

Here is how we say it.

```
structure NPStruct =
  NP(structure a_N = NumberAsNum()
      structure a_P =
        PON(structure a_N = a_N))
```

140 That looks complicated.

What does

NP(**structure** *a_N* = *NumberAsNum*()
    ...)

mean?

141 This is the easiest part to understand. It says that *NP*'s dependency named *a_N* is satisfied by building a structure using the functor *NumberAsNum*.

How about

PON(**structure** *a_N* = *a_N*)?

142 This says that *PON*'s dependency named *a_N* is *a_N*.

Which *a_N* is that last one?

143 It is the one from the previous expression:

structure *a_N* = *NumberAsNum*(),

which was created using *NumberAsNum*().

What else does *NP*'s dependencies demand?

144 The last requirement is that the type *number* in *a_N* and the type *number* in *a_P* must be equal.

Are they?

145 Yes, because *a_N* is reused to create *a_P* using *PON*.

---

146 Can we build all programs in one expression?

Yes.

---

147 We bet that you never thought there was so much to say about *plus*. Define the functor *TON*, which defines *times*, using the signature *T*.

```
signature T¹ =
  sig
    type number
    val times :
          (number * number) → number
  end
```

Don't forget the sharing constraint.

[1] A better name for this signature would be TIMES_OVER_NUMBER.

Here it is. Now go out to dinner.

```
functor TON(structure a_N : N
            structure a_P : P
            sharing type
              a_N.number
              =
              a_P.number)
 ▷
 T where type number = a_N.number
 =
 struct
   type number = a_N.number
   fun times(n,m)
     = if a_N.is_zero(m)
         then m
         else a_P.plus(n,
                times(n,a_N.pred(m)))
 end
```

Don't forget to leave a tip.

The Tenth Moral

Real programs consist of many components. Specify the dependencies among these components using signatures and functors.

Commencement

You have reached the end of your introduction to computation with types and functions. While computation has been popularized over the past few years, especially by the Web and consumer software, it also has a profound, intellectually challenging side. If you wish to delve deeper into this side of computing, starting from a typed viewpoint, we recommend the following tour:

References

1. Heijenoort. *From Frege to Goedel: A Source Book in Mathematical Logic, 1879–1931.* Harvard Press, 1967.

2. Pierce. *Basic Category Theory for Computer Scientists.* MIT Press, 1991.

3. Girard, Taylor, and Lafont. *Proofs and Types.* Cambridge University Press, 1989.

4. Enderton. *A Mathematical Introduction to Logic.* Academic Press, 1972.

5. Constable et alii. *Implementing Mathematics With the Nuprl Proof Development System.* Prentice Hall, 1986.

If you then wish to explore the definition of ML, you may wish to study:

1. Milner, Tofte, Harper, and MacQueen. *The Definition of Standard ML—Revised.* MIT Press, 1997.

2. Milner and Tofte. *Commentary on Standard ML.* MIT Press, 1991.

Index

This is for the loyal Schemers.

```
signature Ysig
  =
  sig
    val Y :
      ((α → α) → (α → α)) → (α → α)
  end
```

```
functor Yfunc()
  ▷
  Ysig
  =
  struct
    datatype α T = Into of α T → α
    fun Y(f)
          = H(f)(Into(H(f)))
    and H(f)(a)
          = f(G(a))
    and G(Into(a))(x)
          = a(Into(a))(x)
  end
```

```
structure Ystruct
  = Yfunc()
```

No, we wouldn't forget factorial.

```
fun mk_fact(fact)(n)
    = if (n = 0)
        then 1
        else n * fact(n - 1)
```

What is the value of

Ystruct.Y(mk_fact)(10)?